GW00361283

FOR
SUCH A
TIME AS THIS

FOR
SUCH A
TIME AS THIS

THE SOVEREIGNTY AND GOODNESS OF GOD IN

THE BOOK OF ESTHER

Colin Mercer

Copyright © 2019, Colin Mercer

All rights reserved. No part of this book may be reproduced,
scanned, or distributed in any printed or electronic form
without permission.

All Bible quotations are from the Authorized (King James) Version.

First Edition: 2019

ISBN: 978-0-9600203-7-9

Book Design and Cover by:
Great Writing Publications
Taylors, SC, USA
www.greatwriting.org

Appreciations

Esther is fascinating history—a thrilling record of divine providence in the care of His people. Amid the fascination and thrill, its personal and practical richness can be lost. Not so with Colin Mercer. In a warmly pastoral manner, he sets before his audience vivid descriptions of the consequences of godless thinking, and warming scenes of divine mercy. He sees in Esther, and in the world that swirled about her, the sovereign rule of a gracious God, and therefrom makes godly and practical application for every believer. Doubtless this helpful read will be one to which the reader is repeatedly drawn.

—*John McKnight, Minister, Reformation Bible Church, Darlington, Maryland, USA*

The title of this study *For Such a Time as This* is most appropriate. The author rightly comments that these are the most well-known words in the book. They are Mordecai's words, put to Esther in the form of a most personal question—"*And who knoweth whether thou art come to the kingdom for such a time as this?*" The initial chapters of *Esther* lead inexorably to this question; and all that follows flows naturally from it. Very thoughtfully and incisively Rev. Mercer builds his exposition around this question. The result is a very readable and helpful presentation of the meaning and the message of *Esther*. I have read through Rev. Mercer's manuscript with great personal blessing. I count him as a beloved brother in Christ and a personal friend. I congratulate him on a production that will undoubtedly prove to be of great encouragement to Christ's Church.

—*John Greer, Minister, Ballymena Free Presbyterian Church, Northern Ireland*

Contents

Acknowledgements

The content of these chapters was first presented in the morning services in Faith Free Presbyterian Church, Greenville South Carolina, USA. The messages were delivered to encourage God's people and to open up the truths of God's sovereignty and care, even in the darkest times. The preparation and preaching of them thrilled my own soul, and in God's mercy brought a measure of blessing to the congregation. Upon their completion, some dear friends encouraged their publication. My relocation to Northern Ireland hindered any immediate progress in that direction. In time, the burden to publish the messages returned and Charles and Verta Koelsch again offered to help. Their work has been invaluable and very much appreciated. Jim Holmes of Great Writing Publications expressed great enthusiasm for the project and I am indebted to him for his encouragement and guidance. Above all, I am thankful to God for saving me, and putting me into the gospel ministry. His Word is everlastingly precious, and I pray that this brief study of Esther will be profitable to all who read it.

Foreword

So limited is their engagement with Esther that many Bible readers would struggle to recall much more than the fact that this Old Testament book omits the name of God. Let this be clear: The Almighty has no need to write His name in order to show us that He superintends human history! That much is evident in the book of Esther. Here is omniscience anticipating evil, omnipotence frustrating the schemes of the wicked, and providence elevating the righteous at just the right time. Truly, God is at work in these chapters, confirming "His most holy, wise and powerful preserving and governing all His creatures, and all their actions" (*Westminster Shorter Catechism*, Answer 11).

And this golden thread of Divine sovereignty is clearly visible in Colin Mercer's welcome analysis of a much-neglected part of Scripture. But this is no dry and dusty tome! It comes from the pen of a preacher; and its beats are those of a pastor's heart. It seeks to evangelise, with many a warning to the careless sinner— and it aims to edify, with instruction for the Christian in these testing times. Throughout, Mr Mercer combines the virtues of careful exegesis, lucid commentary, and pointed application. If it is easy to read—and that, too, is a virtue—it is not always an easy read, for it challenges, prompting the heart-searching and self-examination required of us all.

One of the old writers tells us that the Jews styled this book *Megillah*, "the roll," since it was always written on a separate roll and read through at the feast of Purim. If we unwind that roll after many centuries, endeavouring to discover its treasures, we shall find Colin Mercer's book just the resource we need to realise our objective.

Timothy Nelson,
Principal, Whitefield College of the Bible and minister of Ballynahinch
Free Presbyterian Church, Northern Ireland

An Overview of Esther

The final chapter of 2 Kings records the devastating overthrow of Jerusalem by Nebuchadnezzar, king of Babylon. In what was the second of two very successful sieges within the space of eleven years, he and his army caused complete havoc in that city. Zedekiah the king of Jerusalem was captured and made to watch his own sons being put to death, before his eyes were put out and he was taken away as a prisoner. The temple, already plundered during a previous attack, was burned and left as a pile of smouldering rubble. The walls of the city were broken down, the gates were burned with fire, and thousands of terrified Jews were taken as captives to Babylon.

This was the time of Israel's captivity—a harrowing experience, a time of uncertainty, and a period of great chastisement and correction. What made that situation worse for the Jews was the fact that it had come about due to their sin against God. However, though they had forgotten God, God had not forgotten them. When His appointed time had come, He moved to have the Jews return to their own land. That plan of restoration involved the overthrow of the Babylonians by the Medes and Persians and the raising up of Cyrus the king of Persia.

When Cyrus was enthroned, he found the Jews still in captivity. He immediately passed a decree, permitting them to return to their own land. Furthermore, he provided them with the financial help they needed to rebuild the temple in Jerusalem. It was a remarkable turn of events. The gold and silver that had been stolen was returned, people were encouraged to contribute to the work, royal decrees were issued, making the transition from Babylon to Jerusalem easier, and everything was carried out with the royal seal of approval.

At that time, almost 50,000 Jews returned to Jerusalem. However, for some reason a large number of Jews decided to remain in Persia. As time marched on, Cyrus died, and Ahasuerus became the king over a dominion that stretched across 127 provinces. The extent of the Persian Empire was immense. It reached from the northern part of Libya in the west, into parts of India in the east.

It was recognised as a great empire—rich, powerful, glorious for its time, and, for many years, seemingly invincible. The Jews who refused to return to Israel had become integrated into the Persian way of life.

All of that is important as we come into the book of Esther, for the events that are recorded here involve those Jews living under this Persian regime. The book details the danger they faced, the mysterious providences of God, the working of all things for their good, the overwhelming mercy of the Lord to His people, and the glorious theme of God remembering His covenant and proving Himself faithful at all times.

Before we examine four great themes in this book, it is good to note that, (a) The book of Esther records events that took place 500 years before the birth of Christ; (b) This book is the only book in the Bible where all of the events take place in Persia; (c) There is no clear statement identifying the author; (d) The book of Esther is, in some circles, often not considered to be a part of Scripture. This view is taken for various reasons, for example: the name of God does not appear in these chapters, there is no direct mention of the Messiah, the book is not quoted in the New Testament, and Christian writers never mentioned it. I counter those arguments by noting that the book of Esther occupies a legitimate place in Scripture and carries a message in accordance with the rest of God's Word. It exalts God, testifies to His power and providence, and reveals that His majesty and sovereignty exceed that of any human king. Esther provides us with a series of powerful, spiritual truths which I trust will instruct, encourage, edify, and challenge hearts. This is an old book with a very up-to-date and timely message. There are four themes that will provide us with a framework as we explore these chapters.

A Sovereign God

Much has been made of the fact that the name of God does not appear in the book of Esther. It is true that there is no direct use of God's name. There is nothing here that addresses God in the usual way that we find Him addressed throughout the rest of the Old Testament. It has been suggested that the name Jehovah is secretly hidden in four places in the original text, in the form of an acrostic. It is claimed that in several ancient manuscripts the consonants that form the name Jehovah are written larger than the other letters, and as they appear in consecutive order, the careful reader can discern the name Jehovah.

Leaving that aside for Hebrew scholars, the name of God is not mentioned in the usual way in this book. This in no way suggests that God is not present. Matthew Henry once wisely wrote these words of Esther: "Though the name of God is not in it, his finger is." In other words, while God does not identify Himself by His name, He does so by His works

The book of Esther is not primarily about Ahasuerus or the Jews. It is not pre-eminently about Esther or Mordecai. They all play an important role in the unfolding drama of these chapters, but the book is about God and how He moves and orders His own purposes in the lives of men and women. God was not a mere spectator of life in Persia. He was not looking at events in the empire from afar, like someone visiting Facebook just to see what everyone else is doing but with no real connection with, and no real input into, their lives. God was at work. He was raising people up and putting people down. He was orchestrating events according to His own plan. He was putting people where He wanted them to be at the right time and fulfilling His own eternal decrees for His own eternal glory. While Ahasuerus was ruling over Persia, God was ruling over him.

When man reads this book, he sees intrigue, mystery, chance encounters, accidents, and fortunate or unfortunate circumstances. He sees things that appear out of control. Yet nothing could be further from the truth. While man was not in control, God was, and He remains in control. Let us never lose sight of that. There is a grave temptation in these days to think that the world is in sheer chaos. Are we out of control? For a Christian, the question is a bad one, for we know that He is in control and that

> *God moves in a mysterious way*
> *His wonders to perform.*

We should not question the sovereignty of God just because our little minds cannot comprehend the sovereignty of God. The book of Esther reveals:

THE PRECISION OF GOD'S SOVEREIGNTY

God does not just control the big things in life; He controls all things. In Esther 6 we read of a night in which the king could not sleep. It looks like a throwaway statement, but in a very real sense the book hinges on statements like this. That sleepless night was no accident. It was not just a bad night for Ahasuerus. God took sleep from him and, from there onwards, the plan to destroy the Jews unravelled at an alarming rate. God was at work in the night as well as the day. Everything was under His precise control.

THE PERFECTION OF GOD'S SOVEREIGNTY

Everything God does is right. He never has to undo something in order to correct a failure. He has no Plan B—because His Plan A never fails. What He wills to do, He does. Every detail is right.

THE POWER OF GOD'S SOVEREIGNTY

Ahasuerus was the king of a vast and victorious empire, the most powerful man in the world, but not more powerful than God. God's work was irresistible. No one could stop His plan being fulfilled.

THE PURPOSE OF GOD'S SOVEREIGNTY

In a sentence, God's purposes revolve primarily for His own glory and the good of His own people.

Christians can take tremendous encouragement from that. Is it not strange that we can trace the hand of God in history and we can believe the promise of God in prophecy, but somehow, we think He is not in control right now? God is in control of the smallest details of our lives. He who numbers the hairs of our head orders every event in our lives. "The Lord God omnipotent reigneth" (Revelation 19:6).

A SPECIAL PEOPLE

From a human perspective, the contrast between the Persians and the Jews was huge. The Persians were powerful, and they had defeated the Babylonians and were ready to go into Greece. They were in their own land and had riches and authority over those around them. However, the Jews were second-generation exiles; they were surrounded by strangers and in a foreign land. They knew that, at any moment, they could be rounded up, their property taken from them, and they would lose everything. To look at the Jews in Persia you could almost be forgiven for thinking there was nothing significant about them. That would be to reckon without God.

The Jews were *God's covenant people*. In Genesis 12, God said to Abram, "Get thee out of thy country, and from thy kindred, and from thy father's house, unto a land that I will shew thee: And I will make of thee a great nation, and I will bless thee, and make thy name great; and thou shalt be a blessing: And I will bless them that bless thee, and curse him that curseth thee: and in thee shall all families of the earth be blessed."

God had covenanted to take care of His people and nothing had changed that covenant pledge. The Jews were a chosen people—a special nation in the sight of God. We must remember that God's covenant promise was Christ centred. The Messiah would come through the line of David and therefore the preservation of the Jews throughout the centuries was crucial. The overarching message of Esther is that God cares for His own people and that His care is clearly revealed in the person and work of His Son Jesus Christ.

This is a comforting truth for every believer in Christ. Our acceptance and blessing by God is based on His covenant and, as such, it is steadfast and unchangeable, even when we sin against Him. Christ is the Mediator of this covenant, therefore the Christian is safe and secure in Christ. God does not deal with us in unloving or unfatherly ways because of our foolishness and weakness. He loves His people with an everlasting love and, while that love often involves chastisement and correction, He will spare us and take care of us for His own name's sake. God did not forsake the Jews in Persia, and He has promised never to leave or forsake His people today. He cares for His own on covenant terms, and He is ever mindful of that covenant.

A Sinful Society

The Persian empire was not a spiritual or God-fearing empire. Its society was as sinful as any empire before it or after it. Drunkenness, immorality, pride, treachery, murder, dishonesty, pagan worship, covetousness, lying, and a disregard for God and man were all part of daily life. King Ahasuerus was a leading figure in all that was wicked and sinful. He was a bloodthirsty man with an imperious temper. Yet God's people were preserved in the midst of that kind of society.

When I read of what took place in those days, I see a parallel with what takes place in our own day. These are immoral times. Sadly, debauchery and depravity are not kept for dark alleys and private rooms; instead, they are openly paraded. Immortality is the stuff of entertainment; pornography has invaded homes and destroys men, women, marriages, and families; drunkenness and drug addiction are common; profane language, dishonesty, cheating, lying and jealously are the order of the day. Children rebel against parents and parents are at war with each other. Family life, so often viewed as the fabric of society, has unravelled and marriages are collapsing; purity, honesty, and decency are counted for little and there is a perilous tide of wickedness and godlessness. Ahasuerus is dead and in his own place—but the spirit he lived by is alive and well, and as we continue towards the Lord's return, men will become worse and worse. Let us understand the times, know our responsibility, and remember that God will take care of His people. We are not the first believers to live in days like these.

A SAVING PURPOSE

This is a book about preservation—the preservation of God's people. Although Haman had hatched a plan against the Jews, God was for them and, in His time, and according to His ways, He delivered them.

Throughout the Scriptures we are reminded that Christ will have His people with Him in glory. Things may look bad now, but the end is not yet, and the best is yet to be.

The book of Esther is a thrilling book; full of practical instruction, encouraging truth, divine providences, and an eternal plan that cannot fail. It is God's plan for His people in Christ.

1

A Window into the Sinner's World

Now it came to pass in the days of Ahasuerus...

Esther 1:1,2

The rise of the Persian Empire (approximately 500 years before the birth of Christ) marked a phenomenal turning point in the history of the Jewish people. Prior to those days, thousands of Jews had been taken captive from Jerusalem and were living as exiles in Babylon. Their homeland lay in ruins. The walls of Jerusalem had been broken down. The great temple had been ransacked. A whole generation of young people had been removed, and the future seemed extremely bleak and absolutely hopeless.

Then God moved against the Babylonians and raised up a Persian King called Cyrus. Daniel chapter five records a dramatic night in Babylon when it describes a great feast that Belshazzar of Babylon hosted for a thousand of his lords. In usual Babylonian glory, Belshazzar's feast was a lavish affair. He called for the golden goblets that had been stolen from the temple in Jerusalem, and he and his guests spent the night drinking wine and worshipping their worthless idols.

It was a night which involved the king's wives, princes, nobles and officers of the realm. But the revelry was interrupted by a strange and miraculous event—for at the height of the feasting, the fingers of a man's hand appeared and began to write on the wall beside a candlestick. Imagine the impact the appearance of those fingers made upon all who were gathered in the great hall. The king saw them, and, as he watched those fingers engrave words into the plaster, the expression on his face changed. He began to shake. His strength left him. He was not able to control himself, and then he cried out for men to come and explain the writing on the wall. At that point he had no idea what the words *"mene -mene tekel u-phar-sin"* meant.

Wise men were summoned, and although they were deemed the wisest in the nation, they could not tell Belshazzar what the writing was all about. At last Daniel the prophet of the Lord indicated that he could explain the writing, and when he was brought in, he told the king that he had been weighed in the balances and found wanting, that his days were numbered, and that his kingdom would be given to the Medes and Persians. Belshazzar may or may not have believed Daniel; but before that night was over, the king was dead, and the Medes had taken his kingdom.

Everything was changed. One empire had fallen and another had risen. One king was gone; another was on the throne. The Babylonians, who once thought themselves invincible, had been defeated, and a new world power was in place. It is the way of the world. God causes kingdoms to come and go, and kings to rise and fall. In the course of time, Cyrus became the king of Persia.

By all accounts, Cyrus was not a typical world ruler or military dictator. It is recorded that he entered Babylon in peace amid much rejoicing and jubilation. It is said that his conquest did not follow the normal pattern of those days. Cities were not destroyed, temples or palaces were not razed to the ground, there was no reckless slaughter of people, and he did everything he could to win the favour of the population around him. In one account it is reported that he concerned himself with the internal affairs of Babylon and all of its cities. And that he repaired the homes of the people and freed them from the bondage that many of them were in. He was a different kind of man, a different kind of king. With Cyrus as King of Persia, things changed dramatically for the Jews. Almost as soon as he came to power, Cyrus passed a decree allowing the Jews to return to Jerusalem and rebuild their temple. He also provided the necessary means to make that rebuilding work possible. This was the very thing Isaiah had prophesied some years earlier. In Isaiah 44:28 the Lord said of Cyrus, "He is my shepherd, and shall perform all my pleasure: even saying to Jerusalem, Thou shalt be built; and to the temple, Thy foundation shall be laid." Remarkable as it seems to us, God used this man to bring about the restoration of His people from captivity. However, not all of them took up that offer.

After several years on the throne Cyrus died, and eventually his grandson, the king whose name appears at the beginning of the book of Esther, came to the throne of Persia. There was a great contrast between Cyrus and Ahasuerus. Cyrus was tolerant, quiet, considerate, calm, peaceable—not a godly man but helpful, and used of God to bring great change for the Jews. Ahasuerus, on the other hand, had an impatience about him. At times he was ruthless, thoughtless, careless and lacking in good judgment. One person made the point that, "morally he was a mixture of passionate extremes."

Ahasuerus was a complex character. Often rash, not one given to taking advice well, he was a changeable, fickle, and unstable king. Esther chapter one looks into his world. It was a godless world, full of short-lived pleasure and deep-rooted problems; a world of sin and depravity and reckless decisions; a world of vanity and emptiness; a world where worldly wisdom was seen in all of its hopelessness and worthlessness—and as such it provides a picture of the world of the sinner in our own generation.

This is one of the striking things about Scripture. While it records historical events and shows us things from a previous age, its message is right up to date. The details that are recorded in Esther chapter one read like a commentary on events that take place in our day. What is this world of ours like? How do people live? What's their focus? What is wrong with sinners and with society? This chapter provides a window with a vivid view into the sinner's world. There are three noteworthy observations:

THE WRONG PRIORITY OF THE SINNER

Even the most casual reading of Esther 1 reveals just what it was that Ahasuerus and his friends lived for. These verses highlight what was important to them, what motivated them, what really mattered to them. It does not take a genius to see that there was nothing godly or spiritual here. King Ahasuerus had no time for true religion. He was a self-centred, sin-loving, sensually driven man. Although great responsibilities lay upon him, he lived for the flesh and was consumed with the empty and vain things of the world. Look at the details:

HE FOCUSED ON PLEASURE.

Esther 1 is the chapter of three feasts (vv. 3, 5, and 9). These were no ordinary banquets. The first one lasted 180 days, and another one lasted seven days. That particular feast was held in the most lavish of surroundings. No expense was spared, and as v. 7 records, they drank wine (the best royal wine) out of distinctly different golden goblets. Some commentators say that the words mean no two drinking glasses were the same; others say that no man drank wine out of the same glass twice. Whatever the way of it, it was a lavish affair. The wine flowed. (The word "feast" in vv. 3, 5, and v. 9, points to a drinking feast.) The party spirit was in full swing. Pleasure was the key thing. It was seven days of living it up: eating, drinking, and being merry.

Does that not sound like a worldly man's dream? This is what many sinners live for. They go to work all week so they can party all weekend—and that is no exaggeration. I have listened to radio programmes in which young eighteen-year-olds were interviewed and stated that is how they spent their time. Others might not go to that length, but their focus is on having a good time: living it up, with enjoyment, pleasure, and fun. There is no consideration given to serious things. This is a pleasure-driven world. Perhaps there are some like that who are now reading this book.

HE FOCUSED ON POWER.

Ahasuerus was the king of a vast realm. The Persian Empire was huge. It had swallowed up kingdoms and had grown larger and more powerful. But it is claimed that the feast that is mentioned in Esther 1 took place before the Persian army went out against Greece. This is why v. 3 records that the feast involved "all his princes and servants; the power of Persia and Media, the nobles and princes of the provinces." He had gathered these men together to gain their support for his upcoming campaign in Greece. What was Ahasuerus' goal with that campaign? He was trying to extend his kingdom. He wanted to stretch his rule across greater borders. He craved even more power. If he was a pleasure-driven man, he was also a power-driven man, full of pride and living with the idea that he had the right to do as he pleased. Does that sound familiar? Man is full of himself. He has a made a little god out of his own life. He wants to be the king of his own little kingdom, and he wants others to submit to him. The sinner is proud by nature: self-centred and full of self-importance.

HE FOCUSED ON POSSESSIONS.

Look closely at the words of Esther 1:4: "He showed the riches of his glorious kingdom." That is a statement of affluence and wealth. The word "riches" comes from a word that means to accumulate, and clearly the thought is that Ahasuerus had been accumulating wealth throughout his reign. This was important to him. A man may be wealthy and not really care much for it—but not this man. As far as he was concerned, life revolved around his possessions. And that is how it is with many people. Why is the lottery so popular? Why do people get excited when the jackpot runs into millions? Why do people dream of becoming millionaires? Why? Because we live in a world consumed with things. There is nothing wrong with having a nice home, car, or being able to afford a mobile phone or a tablet or any other electronic device. Money is not the root of all evil. But as Paul says in 1 Timothy 6:10, the *love* of money is. And millions of people think they can buy themselves happiness by buying themselves what they want. Possessions are their priority and their god.

HE FOCUSED ON POPULARITY.

Ahasuerus had friends, and I sense as I read these verses that he wanted to show himself friendly. In other words, he craved popularity. This is confirmed in v. 3 when we read, "In the third year of his reign, he made a feast unto all his princes and his servants; the power of Persia and Media, the nobles and princes of the provinces, being before him. When he shewed the riches of his glorious kingdom and the honour of his excellent majesty many days, even an hundred and fourscore days." It seems Ahasuerus wanted to impress!

These are the things that stimulated, excited, and motivated Ahasuerus. It was all worldly and full of vanity! What a way to live life. No mention of God. No reference to the soul. No thought of death or judgment or eternity. No consideration given to standing before God. Just live for the here and now!

THE WRETCHED MISERY OF THE SINNER

At first glance, it looks as if Ahasuerus had it made. According to the world's reckoning, if any man should have been happy, he should have been that man. But when we probe below the surface of his life, when we look a little deeper into this chapter, we discover the wretched misery that accompanies sin and the emptiness of a life without the Lord. Follow the narrative carefully and note the following:

A LIFE OF SIN IS MARKED WITH DISSATISFACTION.

Look at Ahasuerus. He was the king over 127 provinces, yet he was preparing to fight against Greece. He had a feast that lasted six months and then immediately ordered another one for seven days. He had shown his friends his riches and the glory of his kingdom. But then he felt it necessary to command his wife to come so that he could show her off as well. What does all this tell you about him? What kind of man does these things? What was wrong with him? This tells me that Ahasuerus was not a happy man. Nothing really satisfied him. He was not content. He always had to go further.

The truth is that a life of sin cannot truly satisfy. It has been wisely said, "There is a want in the soul of man which all the wealth of one hundred and twenty-seven provinces cannot supply. There is a want which the best social arrangements cannot supply. There is a craving in the heart of man beyond all creature power to satisfy."[1] And it is true. The sinner is never content. He thinks that if he had more money, more freedom—if he could fulfill his dreams; if he had a better job, a newer car, a nicer home, a better spouse, a better family, a better whatever—he would be content. He is always looking for something else because what he is living for can never satisfy him. Consider the lifestory of the prodigal son as recorded in Luke 15. He got his inheritance, went away from home, lived a sinful and sensual life, and spent all that he had, but was left destitute and dissatisfied. Some young people think that if only they could get away from home, things would be better. However, nothing and no one but Christ can satisfy the soul!

THE WORLD'S PLEASURES ARE SHORT LIVED.

In v. 10 we are told that the "the heart of the king was merry with wine." This second feast had been going on for seven days. The king was intoxicated, and in that state he was arrogant and bold towards his wife. He asked her to come before him so that he might show her off to his drinking friends. As v. 11 notes, he wanted "to shew the people and the princes her beauty: for she was fair to look on." The word "shew" is the same word that is used in v. 4, where it records that "he shewed the riches of his glorious kingdom." In his drunken state, he treated Vashti like an object and wanted her to stand before his party friends so that men could gape at her. He had no respect for his wife. What right-thinking man would want to bring his beautiful wife into that kind of situation? Ahasuerus was thinking only of himself. He was not protective of his wife. Matthew Henry said of this that he

...diminished himself as a king, in commanding that from his wife which she might refuse, much to the hon-

1 Alexander D Davidson—Biblical Illustrator, cited as *Lectures, Expository and Practical, on the Book of Esther*, https://books.google.com/books?id=36UCAAAAQAAJ

our of her virtue. It was against the custom of the Persians for the women to appear in public, and he put a great hardship upon her when he did not court, but command her to do so uncouth a thing, and make her a show.

He was consumed with the outward and fleshly things of life. It was all for him. This was worse than foolish. He sent for her, but she refused. Then v. 12 tells us that he was very wroth and his anger burned within him. Ahasuerus fell into a rage. His drinking turned him into a monster. George Lawson said, "Wine has transformed him from a king to a clown, or something below a clown." One minute he was merry—and the next minute he was mad! His feel-good factor did not last very long. The pleasure he had from his ungodly feast and among his ungodly friends did not even see him through the night! Let us understand this: the pleasures of the world, no matter what kind they are, are short lived. They last for a very little time. They are like the bubbles that children blow. They look good, then burst.... But the gospel brings everlasting benefits—eternal blessings. The godless things of this world are temporary.

THE WAYS OF THE WORLD ARE THE WAYS OF DESTRUCTION AND RUIN.

Ponder what happened that night. Ahasuerus called for Vashti to come. It was a reckless request. He wanted to parade her as a trophy before his officers. But she refused, and the upshot of that refusal was that he divorced her! (There is a debate as to whether Vashti was right or wrong in not obeying her husband. Some commentators argue that she should have complied; others take a different view. It may be she should have tried at least to communicate with him—or try to diffuse the situation in a different way—but her refusal was direct and determined, and the whole event ended in divorce.) What started out as a merry feast ended with a man set against his wife and a wife set against her husband. The marriage was broken. The union was dissolved. The home was destroyed. No wonder George Lawson once said, "A curse is mingled with all the prosperity of sinners, because they know not how to use or to enjoy, but are disposed, by their corrupt tempers, to abuse everything which they possess." The way of sin was the way of ruin. The night ended with the destruction of a marriage. There is nothing but ruin in these verses.

And I can come to no other conclusion as I read this chapter, but that drink contributed to the catastrophe. Matthew Henry said of Ahasuerus. "If he had not been put out of the possession of himself by drinking to excess, he would not have done such a thing, but would have been angry at any one that should have mentioned it. When the wine is in the wit is out, and men's reason departs from them." It would have been far better for Ahasuerus and Vashti if he had never taken the first glass of wine—better for him if he had abstained.

Let that be a warning to every person reading these words. Many a life and marriage has been destroyed by a drunken husband. Many a home is on the rocks because the warning signs have been ignored. Many a life has been ruined by alcohol. I'm not suggesting for one moment that every problem in home life can be traced back to this, for that is obviously not the case. But there are many cases where families have been ruined because drink was introduced to the home. Many a home has been destroyed by other addictions such as drugs (even prescription drugs) and pornography and selfishness. Be warned!

What is for sure, however, is that sin lay at the heart of the devastation of the king's family. The way of the sinner is hard. The devil always brings ruin and destruction. The sinner's world is not one of lasting happiness. Sin is not the happy thing many think it is.

THE WORLDLY FOLLY OF THE SINNER

Ahasuerus was now facing a huge problem. How was he to deal with his wife? His reputation was in jeopardy. What would people think of him? What would this do for others in the nation? He had been publicly slighted by his beautiful wife. What could he do? Verse 12 records his initial reaction. The king was very wroth, and his anger burned within him. It was going from bad to worse.

There was no calm reflection, no second thoughts, and no pulling back. He flew into a burning rage. Then he called his advisors and asked them what to do. On the surface this may look positive as he was asking men who knew the law of the land. However, there were outstanding failures here. For example, he did not search his own heart. There is no record that Ahasuerus engaged in any measure of self-examination. He did not ask, "Was I wrong? Did I do something foolish?" Rather, he said, as Scripture records, "What shall we do unto the queen Vashti according to law?" He put all the blame on his soon-to-be ex-wife. Furthermore, while he sought counsel from men, he did not seek the counsel of godly men. Moreover, he did not turn to the Word of God.

To whom can the sinner turn in times of trouble? Turning to the wisdom of mere men will often only mean that things will go from bad to worse. The greatest needs of the human heart are too deep and too detailed for people to grapple with. Sin is too serious an issue for human answers. Only Christ has the answer for the misery and destructiveness of sin. It is Christ who says, "Come unto me all ye that labour and are heavy laden and I will give you rest." Christ is able to meet the need of those who are sinking in sin. It is pride and worldly folly that keeps the sinner from repenting and seeking His mercy and intervention. Every one of us needs Christ as Saviour and Lord. Thankfully, He is able, ready, and willing to save all who call upon Him for salvation.

The window into the sinner's world reveals a world of rebellion and ruin. Christ Jesus is the only answer to that.

2

The Right Woman

And he brought up Hadassah, that is, Esther, his uncle's
daughter: for she had neither father nor mother, and the
maid was fair and beautiful; whom Mordecai, when her
father and mother were dead, took for his own daughter.

Esther 2:7

Esther 1 closes with Ahasuerus, the reckless king of Persia, passing judgment on his wife and banishing her from the royal court for the rest of her life. His decision to divorce her had come at a time when he had been drinking, at a time when his pride had been hurt, and at a time when he was full of anger and bitterness. Vashti's only crime was refusing to obey her drunken husband when he commanded her to come to his feast so that he could show her off to his friends.

It was an absurd demand that he had made of her, and while Vashti could have reacted differently, and perhaps could have tried to defuse the situation, her refusal to appear did not merit the immediate and irreversible breakup of her marriage. Aha-suerus had acted wrongly in commanding her to come, and he acted just as wrongly in demanding her to leave. This man's wild and impulsive behaviour had not been good for him or for his marriage.

Shortly afterwards, Ahasuerus left Shushan and led a military campaign against Greece.

Between Esther 1 and Esther 2, there is a three or four-year period (we learn that from the words of 1:3 and 2:16), and during that time Ahasuerus had tried to extend his kingdom. Probably, he believed it was a foregone conclusion that he would be suc-cessful. Historians speak of him using tens of thousands of sol-diers, having his navy in place, and anticipating a swift victory. But his campaign to overcome Greece ended in failure. So, he returned to his palace with his tail between his legs. Of course, there was no Vashti to console him—no wife to encourage him.

It seems from Esther 2:1 that, in the midst of those circum-stances, Ahasuerus began to regret what had happened three or four years earlier when he had put Vashti away. The word "re-membered" carries the thought of affectionate remembrance, and it appears that he was grieved and troubled at what he had done. He *remembered* that night when he had sent for her. He *remembered* her refusal to come. He *remembered* the counsel from his advisors. He *remembered* his decree that stated that Vashti would never come before him again and that her royal estate should be given to another. *He remembered* that his law had been sent throughout the Empire and that it was viewed to be unchangeable. *He remembered it all*, and now he knew that he had made a terrible error of judgment. But the law was the law, and even the king was forced to live within it. These opening words paint a scene of regret.

Sin is often followed by despair and regret. And to keep with the tragic circumstances in Esther 1, it is worth noting that many a husband has reason to regret how he has treated his wife. There are men who have no idea what Paul meant when he wrote in Ephesians 5, "Husbands love your wives, even as Christ loved the church, and gave himself for it." They are unfair in their love, unbecoming in their language, unreasonable in their demands, and uncaring in their ways. They take little interest in the needs of their wife. They do not show much affection towards her. They do not pay her much attention. They rarely give her a compliment. They take what they want, but rarely give her what she needs. And if children are involved, often a careless husband has little to do with them. Sadly, things start to fall apart. The selfishness of the husband leads to sadness in the wife. If the marriage continues, it continues in name only. Then something happens. The husband wakes up and sees the error of his ways and regrets his past behaviour. But for some it is almost too late. The damage is almost irreparable. It is tragic. Such a situation can be recovered by the application of the gospel. When there is repentance and restoration, there is hope for marriages that are in trouble. It would have been far better if Ahasuerus had not treated his wife as he did. This was a tragic domestic situation played out in the full glare of the nation, and none of it was good. Husbands should learn from this sad event in Persia. Love your wife, not as King Ahasuerus loved his wife—but as Christ loves His church.

So, Ahasuerus was alone. It was at this critical time in his life that his servants intervened again and suggested that he should take another wife. What these men were proposing was anything but pure and proper. Their plan was that the king would appoint officers in all of the kingdom (across the 127 provinces) to gather up all the young virgins of the realm, bring them back to Shushan, place them under the supervision of Hege (one of the king's eunuchs), and give them twelve months to pamper and prepare themselves for a night with the king. Whichever one would please him the most would become his wife. The others would remain within the palace confines and be numbered among his concubines. These must be viewed as grim details.

It may be that the king's servants suggested this to secure their own safety. After all, they had recommended that Ahasuerus should remove his wife back in Esther 1, and he was now having second thoughts. Perhaps they felt their lives were in danger, and so they proposed this plan to appease the king. Certainly these men thought this would make the king happy. Such thinking still prevails in the minds of men and women. There is a belief that lust and pleasure are key to true happiness. However, it is a sinful and empty way to think. As Solomon discovered, it will be found to be vanity of vanities and vexation of spirit.

There was nothing honourable or respectable in this scheme. What did it say about the sanctity of marriage? What would it do to the young girls brought into the royal court? What kind of message did it give to the men of the kingdom? It was an unjust plan. However, as v. 4 states, "the thing pleased the king," and therefore it was implemented.

The first four verses of Esther 2 are taken up with the affairs of the Persian court. They are about the Gentile king and his lustful ways. But in v. 5, we have a sudden change, and for the first time in the book we are introduced to a Jew. In the verses that follow, our attention is drawn away from Ahasuerus and his life to Mordecai and his adopted daughter, Esther, who are used of God to save the Jews from certain destruction. We must take a little time to examine Esther as she appears in this chapter, and as we do so there are four things we need to ponder.

ESTHER'S BACKGROUND

There is much we do not know about Esther. For example, we do not know about her extended family, although v. 7 records that her mother and father were both dead. We do not know her exact age. Some commentators speculate that she may have been in her late teens or early twenties. We do not know if she worked or what she did in Shushan. These details are not provided. But there are details here that give us a glimpse into her background, and all of them are important.

THE SIGNIFICANCE OF HER TWO NAMES

According to v. 7, her Hebrew name was Hadassah and her Persian name was Esther. The name Hadassah means myrtle and comes from the name of the myrtle plant that was so common in Israel during Bible times. It was an evergreen plant which in summer produces flowers, followed by black berries. According to some studies, when the shrub is burned and grows again, many of its leaves appear in clusters of three. While it was a common shrub, it was also very significant, for Isaiah spoke of it in connection with the restoration of Israel. In Isaiah 55:13 he said, "Instead of the thorn shall come up the fir tree, and instead of the brier shall come up the myrtle tree: and it shall be to the LORD for a name, for an everlasting sign that shall not be cut off." Similar words appear in Isaiah 41. They concern the revival and return of Israel. The myrtle tree was associated with the end of captivity and the restoration of the Lord's people. It may be that Hadassah's parents looked forward to the day when Israel would be completely restored. Possibly, they were looking for the Lord's blessing upon His people, and so they named their daughter Hadassah, or Myrtle, with that promise in mind. Certainly, this young woman was planted in Persia for a particular purpose.

Her other name, *Esther,* is also significant. It comes from a word that means star. Stars are in the heavens and are seen in the darkness of the night. They are used for direction. They give hope. They let a traveller chart a right course.

If the name myrtle makes us think of a plant in the ground, then the name Esther makes us think of that which is in the heavens, and this presents us with a picture of the believer. Christians are citizens of heaven, but we live here on earth, and while we are here, we are to shine as lights, as stars in a dark world. So would be the case with Esther. She was going to perform a vital work in the midst of the darkness of Persia. She was going to be used of God among His people. Her names are significant.

ESTHER WAS NO STRANGER TO TRAGEDY AND DEATH.

Esther 2:7 records that both her father and mother were dead. It is speculated by some that her father died when his wife was expecting their daughter and that her mother died shortly after giving birth. Scripture is silent on that. However, it is true to say that Esther was no stranger to trials. There she was in a foreign land, living under a foreign power. Her father, whose name *Abihail* means might or force, was gone. Her mother was gone, too, and she was an orphan. Few young people could ever understand what that must have been like. But God was in control of all these things. Those trials were preparing her for an even greater trial, and she was going to discover that just as God had not forsaken her when her parents died, so He was not going to forsake her now when death was in the air again.

ESTHER EXPERIENCED THE BLESSING OF ADOPTION.

Verse seven tells us that her cousin, Mordecai, took her as his own daughter. Whether this was a formal adoption or not, the fact is Esther was taken care of. She was brought into a loving situation and provided for and protected by another. There is a glorious picture of the adoption that the believer experiences when he is brought into the family of God. Esther was now under the care and love of another.

None of these things was incidental. God had ordered these various aspects of Esther's life. Her life, her background, even her upbringing were under the superintendence of the Lord, and He had a tremendous purpose for her life. It is the same for all of His people. Romans 8:28 confirms the point – "And we know that all things work together for good, to them that love God, to them who are the called according to his purpose."

ESTHER'S BEAUTY

It is almost impossible to read Esther 2, and the details of the plan to find another wife for Ahasuerus, and not notice the emphasis that was placed on the outward beauty of the young girls. Consider the reference in v. 3 to "fair young virgins." The word "fair" means good to look at, good in appearance. Verse 3 further adds, "Let their things for purification be given them." That is explained in the words of v. 12, where it speaks of six months of oil of myrrh treatments and six months of perfumes and other beauty products. There was a quest to find the most beautiful girls in the kingdom. And Esther was among them. We learn from v. 7 that: "...the maid was fair and beautiful." Those are significant terms. They mean that Esther was a very attractive person. An alternative phrase could be that she was "fair of form and good of countenance." Esther was a beautiful girl. She was right up there with the rest of them when it came to physical appearance. But that is not all. While Esther had outward beauty, she also had an inward beauty. The details of the chapter confirm this: she was pleasant and winsome. In v. 9, we are told that she pleased Hegai, the keeper of the women. Adam Clarke suggested this was probably because of "the propriety of her deportment, and her engaging though unassuming manners." Esther was a pleasant person.

Furthermore, she was submissive and obedient. Mordecai was her adopted father, and she accepted his advice and counsel. She honoured him. Esther 2:10 highlights that she obeyed Mordecai when he charged her not to reveal that she was a Jewess.

She was modest and reserved. According to v. 15 when it was her turn to go in before the king, "she required nothing"; that is, nothing to make her more beautiful or more appealing or more attractive. She was content as she was. This was Esther's real beauty. Matthew Henry said, "Her wisdom and virtue were her greatest beauty." And that is the most important kind of beauty.

The court of Ahasuerus was interested only in the outward appearance of these girls. There was no reference to their inner beauty. The king was not concerned with character, with personalities, with skills or with talents. There was no real regard for the women themselves. This, too, is an age where physical beauty is considered to be all important. Images of models appear everywhere—many of them photoshopped to look differently. Glossy pictures in magazines give the impression that you must have good looks, be a certain size, and be attractive to others if you are going to succeed. The inference is that if you are not like that, you are not good enough. This unscriptural mindset places girls under incredible pressure. We must remember, it is God who forms us; we are the work of His hands. Psalm 139:14, 15 reminds us that we are fearfully and wonderfully made in the womb, and then v. 16 adds that "Thine eyes did see my substance yet being unperfect; and in thy book all my members were written, which in continuance were fashioned, when as yet there was none of them." It is God who fashions us, and He fashions us all differently. But He fashions us according to His sovereign purpose. We have the physical appearance that God desires us to have.

Girls, especially, should try to understand that. If you are a woman, do not be jealous of another who appears more beautiful than you. You are made as God would have you to be. Remember, there is a beauty that is more important that outward appearance. Peter addressed that matter in 1 Peter 3 when he spoke of the beauty of a "meek and quiet spirit." This is true beauty: the beauty of godliness, the beauty of a genuine Christlikeness, the beauty of a godly character. This is far more important than the values of beauty the world lives by. Nurture a Christlikeness that will glorify God and that will be a blessing to yourself and others.

Esther's Behaviour

This brings us into some of the more difficult aspects of this chapter. Usually, three questions surround Esther's presence in the palace. Was she right to take part in this beauty contest? Was she right to conceal the fact that she was a Jew? Was she right to go into the king and spend a night with him? Those are tough questions. Let's consider each one.

ESTHER'S PRESENCE IN THE PALACE

How did she come to be there at all? She did not simply offer herself. She was there by the king's decree: there are references to the "king's commandment and decree" (Esther 2:3, 4, 8). This was the law of the Persian king. Officers were sent, "to gather (to grasp or collect) together" (v. 3) "all the young virgins." There were no exceptions. The verb "gathered" in v. 8 is in the passive tense, signifying that the young virgins did not gather themselves; they were gathered by others. Then they were "brought unto the king's house." The word "brought" can have the idea of being carried away. It seems from the language of these verses that Esther had no option. Some preachers have accused her of offering no resistance. Some have said the same of Mordecai, that he raised no voice of protest. But we must remember the customs and cultures of that day. There was no choice in this. We do not read that the king's officers asked these young women to come; rather, that they brought them.

ESTHER'S SILENCE IN THE PALACE

Why did she not reveal that she was a Jew? Why did she obey her cousin Mordecai? After all, Daniel and his friends made it clear that they were Jews when they were in Babylon (Daniel 1). Why not Esther? It could also be alleged that she must not have looked or acted as a Jewess, since no question was raised regarding her nationality. Was this a sign that she had forsaken the laws of God while living in Persia? Scripture is silent on these matters, so we must be careful. It may be that she was afraid for her life or it may be that Mordecai was led of the Lord to instruct her this way. Perhaps she wanted to fit in with the other girls, though I do not see that in other aspects of her behaviour. In some ways this is a mystery; therefore, we should not take this to be a precedent that we should follow in every situation. In the providence of God, she revealed her Jewishness at a future time.

ESTHER'S COMPLIANCE IN THE PALACE

Remember, once she was in the palace, there was no going back home. This beauty contest was on strange terms. If you pleased the king you became his wife; if you did not please him, you went into his harem and became one of his concubines. It seems from v. 15 that Esther made no special effort for the king, and there is no comment that she enjoyed any of this, but in the providence of God she was chosen. This is a difficult part of the book. It certainly does not give licence for this type of behaviour. Ahasuerus was a sinful man and the scheme he embarked on was perverse and without any scriptural warrant. It appears that Esther was in a situation that she had no control over and that she sought to make the best of that situation. What we do know is that God was overruling all of this. Esther was where God providentially wanted her to be. Her life had to be preserved because she was going to be instrumental in preserving the lives of others. While we may conclude that Esther did not do all things well, we know that God does.

ESTHER'S BLESSING

Though Esther was in an ungodly place and surrounded by ungodly people, there was one man who loved her as his own. Mordecai was sympathetic towards her. He was interested in her welfare. He watched out for her. He counselled her, and he worked for her good. He was a Jew, a despised man, one who remembered the ways of God with His people in the past. And he cared for Esther. The Christian certainly has one who cares for him in all of the twists and turns of life. In Christ, believers have a Friend that sticks closer than a brother, One who is full of grace and wisdom. Indeed, Christ is touched with the feeling of our infirmities. He understands and succours His people in their times of temptation and trials. He has promised never to leave us or forsake us, and we can find the greatest comfort in the knowledge that His grace is always sufficient for us. What a blessing believers have in having Christ.

God was moving in mysterious ways to bring Esther to the throne, for He had a work for her to do. Did she understand that at this point? I do not think so; this was an unseen blessing. Strange circumstances for sure—strange providences in her life. She could never have imagined this course of events, but God had planned it all. What she did not understand to be a blessing, she would understand in time to come. And as it was for Esther, so it will be for all of God's people. There are things that happen to us, and they look mysterious and out of control. They are anything but out of control. God is in sovereign control of every event in this world and every event in our lives. And as the psalmist notes in Psalm 57, He is performing all things for His people

.

3

A Man Called Mordecai

*And Mordecai walked every day before the court of
the women's house, to know how Esther did, and what
should become of her.*

Esther 2:11

We do not have to read too far into the book of Esther to discover that a nation that knows little or nothing of the fear of God will lurch from one great crisis to another. In these opening chapters, we are introduced to life in the Persian Empire around 500 years before the birth of Christ. It was the greatest empire in the world at that time: powerful, wealthy, growing, and apparently invincible. It was the terror of other nations, and it had all the hallmarks of becoming the mightiest empire the world would ever know.

But Persia was a godless place. Its king, Ahasuerus, did not know the Lord, and his officers and advisors were worldly men. There was no reference to the law of God; no gathering for true worship; no humble reverence for God; nothing but a living for self and for the things of the world. In the absence of a true fear of God, the Persian Empire was full of reckless and sinful behaviour.

Huge decisions were taken against a backdrop of drunkenness. It has been said by one historian that the Persians did not make plans or arrangements if they were sober. That point is borne out in Esther 1. Although the king was planning to fight against Greece, he spent the months before that campaign in the midst of a drinking feast. A party spirit dominated life in Persia. There was a careless approach to serious things. Solemn reflection was left for others as the Persians gave themselves to drunkenness.

Remember, Ahasuerus showed a dreadful disregard for the honour of his wife. In Esther 1:4 we read that he had shown his officers the riches of his glorious kingdom. Most likely, he gave these men a tour of his palace and bragged about his wealth. He was a proud man, full of self-importance; and he liked to make much of his wealth. But v. 11 shows how he tried to treat his wife in the same way. He called her to come to his drunken feast so that he could show her off to his men. What man having professed to love his wife would then make her stand so that other men could gape at her? Obviously, Ahasuerus thought he could. There was no love in that command. He had no respect for his wife, no regard for her well-being, and no interest in her safely or dignity. The man was controlled by his own lusts.

Furthermore, Persian culture thought little of the marriage covenant. When Vashti refused to come, Ahasuerus sought counsel from his officers, and they suggested that he divorce her. They argued that if she were to get away with this spirit of disobedience, then no man would be master in his own home, and every woman potentially would rise up and the nation would descend into anarchy. Their advice was short, sharp, and to the point: for the good of the kingdom Vashti must be sent away. So, Ahasuerus sent her away. He thought nothing of breaking his marriage because of one incident. Marriage was cheap in Persia; its covenant meant very little.

There was also an obsession with physical beauty and immoral behaviour. The plan to find another queen was anything but holy or honourable. Young virgin girls who were deemed to be beautiful were rounded up and brought to the palace to be pampered and prepared for a night with the king. The one who pleased him the most became his wife; all the others would be kept as his concubines. It was a wicked scheme and one that was carried out with urgency, but no pity.

The first two chapters of this book leave us with no other option but to conclude that Persia was a godless place. There was no fear of God; and in the absence of a fear of God, all kinds of lusts and sins and debauchery thrived.

Is that not how it is in our generation too? The more a nation argues against and moves away from the teaching of the Scripture, the more it sinks into foul and evil behaviour. When a people reject the Ten Commandments; when they think they have a better way; when they think that God's law is old fashioned and not fit for public consumption; when they think that humanism is better; when they think that man has evolved rather than was created; when they think the gospel is just one of many ways to know God; when they think that man has the right to do whatever is right in his own eyes; when they move away from the Scriptures of God... What happens? They will abandon right for wrong and follow a course of increasing wickedness.

We see it all around us. Nations forget the seventh commandment, "Thou shalt not kill," and they murder thousands of unborn children. They reject the sixth commandment, "Thou shalt not commit adultery," and they set about to destroy the sanctity of marriage. They reject the tenth commandment, "Thou shalt not covet," and they spend their time coveting what others have. A nation that tries to dismantle the Ten Commandments and remove them from public consideration will be a nation that sinks into a state of wild abandonment and spiritual ruin. Persia was like that; and sadly, America and other western nations are becoming more like that, too. It is exactly what the psalmist wrote in Psalm 53 when he noted, "The fool hath said in his heart, there is no God. Corrupt are they, and have done abominable iniquity: there is none that doeth good. Every one of them is gone back: they are altogether become filthy; there is none that doeth good, no, not one." Do you see the connection? The denial of God leads to a life of depravity.

The ancient Persian Empire is a classic example. And yet in the middle of all this wickedness, we discover a Jew called Mordecai and his adopted daughter, Esther, who are used by God to deliver thousands of other Jews from certain destruction. God had mercy on His covenant people. He preserved them, protected them, and fulfilled His ancient promises to them. At the heart of that work, He used this man and this woman for His own glory. Our introduction to Mordecai and his life in Persia presents a number of very important lessons for God's people.

GOD RULES OVER ALL OUR CIRCUMSTANCES ACCORDING TO HIS OWN PURPOSE.

To the casual reader of Scripture, and to the casual observer of history, things just seem to happen by accident. Events and situations and developments are often explained in terms of chance or coincidence. There is a thought that the stuff of life just happens, and no one is in control.

But that is not what the Scriptures teach. In Ephesians 1:11, we read: "In whom also we have obtained an inheritance, being predestinated according to the purpose of him who worketh all things after the counsel of his own will." Acts 2 also addresses the issue of God's determinate counsel; that is, His appointed or decreed counsel. Hebrews 6:17 speaks of "the immutability of his counsel," the fact that it is fixed and settled. What do all those texts mean? They mean that God orders all things.

The Westminster Confession of Faith supports that truth with the statement: "God from all eternity did, by the most wise and holy counsel of His own will, freely, and unchangeably ordain whatsoever comes to pass." In other words, God has ordained all that He will do and all that He permits to be done. This is true of our circumstances. The events of our lives are not haphazard things; they are not random, uncontrolled, or out-of-control incidents. They are not accidents. God is sovereign over them all. A. A. Hodge commented on the confession statement thus: "The plan of God comprehends and determines all things and events of every kind that come to pass." That is well illustrated in the life of Mordecai.

HIS PLACE

Esther 2:5, 6 give us details of Mordecai's family line and links that family to the Babylonian captivity. Verse 5 mentions his father Ja-ir, his grandfather Shimei, and his great-grandfather Kish, who was a Benjamite. (It was this man, Mordecai's great-grandfather, who was carried away captive during the time of King Jeconiah). Clearly, then, Mordecai was born in Persia. He was a second- or third-generation exile. In a sense, he was in Persia because of the sin of an earlier generation of Jews. They had rebelled against God, and God had them taken into captivity. As time passed, Mordecai was born into a captive family line.

It is interesting that he is described as a "Jew." Why not a Hebrew? Why not an Israelite? Why a Jew? Because the title Jew was most commonly used to describe the people of God during their years of captivity. The word Jew or Jews appears over fifty-six times in the Old Testament, and the majority of references have to do with their time in Babylon. It is claimed that the name "Israelite" was only used of the people of Israel when they were in the land of Israel, and the name "Jew" was used when they were outside it.

Therefore, the very fact he is described as Mordecai the Jew makes us think of the sovereignty of God in the captivity of His people. Mordecai's family had been brought to Susa, and for one reason or another he had stayed there when other Jews returned to their homeland. It was not unusual to find a Jew living in the Persian Empire at this time; and this is where Mordecai was. From a human perspective, he should not have been there. The Jews had been given the opportunity to return; but he had stayed. In the overruling providence of God, this man was in Persia at a very critical point in history. God had this man there for a reason.

HIS POSITION

Verse 5 tells us that he was in "Shushan the palace," and v. 11 notes that he had access to the court of the women's house. These words are speaking of the precincts of the royal courts. Mordecai may have been an officer, a public servant of some kind or a royal attendant. In some ways, he was like Obadiah, who served in the court of King Ahab in 1 Kings 17. Mordecai had received a position that enabled him to look out for Esther when she was taken into the palace. God had ordered this. If Mordecai had been in a different position, a different part of the land or a different position in the nation, he could not have been so close to her. This was no accident. He was in the palace because God overruled all things so that he would be there.

His promotion

There is a progression from v. 11 to v. 19 (and v. 21). Mordecai had been promoted to sit at the king's gate. The word "gate" refers to more than just an entrance. The gate was a large and elaborate affair, a place where legal matters were settled. Some commentators think that Mordecai had become a magistrate or a judge. Certainly, the words mean he had some kind of responsibility, civic office, or royal authority. Now, he not only had access to the women's court, but he had access to the entire court. He was in the king's favour, and that promotion was all of God's doing.

None of this was by chance or by mere good fortune. God was superintending all of this. The interesting thing is that there is no explanation given for any of these circumstances. One commentator suggests that Mordecai was in this situation through the influence of Esther; but that is speculation. The Holy Spirit has not given a reason why Mordecai was in this particular situation, and I suggest that is deliberate. If there was an explanation given, then we would attribute these things merely to the plans and purposes of men. What we are being shown here is not the hand of man, but the hand of God. As believers, we must try to understand this. We are where we are in the all-wise and all-perfect providence of God. Our circumstances are under His supervision.

That might raise the question, Why did God allow this? Why were Mordecai and Esther in this situation? Why were they part of a sinful regime, and why did God permit her to be brought unto an immoral king so that she would become his wife? Broaden the question: Why do God's people sometimes find themselves in the midst of very sinful situations, even if it is not their fault? Why does God allow us to sin and sometimes find ourselves in hard positions? That is a good question. The only answer is that God in His sovereignty oversees all the appointments and details of our lives.

That in no way makes Him the author of the sin. The responsibility of the sin lies with the sinner, but God overrules all things for His own glory. A. A. Hodge, in his commentary on the Westminster Confession of Faith, said, "It must be remembered that the purpose of God, with respect to the sinful acts of men and wicked angels is in no degree to cause the evil, nor to approve it, but only to permit the wicked agent to perform it and then to overrule it for His own most wise and holy ends."[2] This is what we learn here. Our circumstances may not always be what we want them to be. They may be hard, difficult, trying, unpleasant, and they may involve sinful people who act in a very sinful way against us. We might not understand the reason behind all of these things, but let us remember that "as for God his way is perfect." God rules over all our circumstances according to His own purpose.

OUR CIRCUMSTANCES PROVIDE AN OPPORTUNITY FOR FAITHFUL SERVICE.

Mordecai was where he was because there was a work for him to do! That much is clear from the record of this chapter. He was not in those positions by accident; therefore, he was there on purpose, and he was given a tremendous opportunity to do good. There are two aspects to this:

HIS REGARD FOR ESTHER

Mordecai's place in the court allowed him to take care of Esther, to counsel her, and to watch over her. If he had been in a different part of the Empire, his involvement with Esther would have been impossible. But God ordered things so that Mordecai would be able to adopt her, advise her, and pay attention to her. We see

---

2   A A Hodge, *The Confession of Faith: A Handbook of Christian Doctrine Expounding the Westminster Confession of Faith*, London, Banner of Truth Trust, 65.

that especially in the words of v. 11: "And Mordecai walked every day before the court of the women's house, to know how Esther did, and what would become of her." Mordecai was concerned for her safety, her health, her welfare, and her peace. He had not forgotten her. He went there every day to enquire after her. In a sense, this was an easy thing for him to do because he was already known in the precincts of the palace. God had put him there. Now he was able to encourage Esther and let her know that though she was in some ways out of sight, she was not out of mind. Mordecai was keen to keep on ministering to her. He could not do much, but he did what he could and he was faithful every day.

His report to Ahasuerus

Pay attention to the words of vv. 21-23. "In those days, while Mordecai sat in the king's gate, two of the king's chamberlains, Bigthan and Teresh, of those which kept the door, were wroth, and sought to lay hand on the king Ahasuerus. And the thing was known to Mordecai, who told it unto Esther the queen; and Esther certified the king thereof in Mordecai's name. And when inquisition was made of the matter, it was found out; therefore they were both hanged on a tree: and it was written in the book of the chronicles before the king." This section is full of intrigue, plots, and murderous intent. Bigthan and Teresh were plotting to assassinate King Ahasuerus. They had grown angry with him, and were ready to murder him. But Mordecai heard of their treacherous and murderous scheme. He was sitting in the gate (again, note, where God had placed him) and became aware of the plan and told it to Esther—who in turn told it to the king—and the plan was thwarted. Mordecai played a vital role in saving the king's life. God had him in a place where he could serve, and Mordecai used the opportunities before him to do good.

There are several points to note with regard to his service: (a) He served according to the law of God. On both these accounts (Esther and Ahasuerus), Mordecai showed that he loved his neighbour as himself. Mordecai's actions in reporting the threat to the king were in keeping with the sixth commandment. When the law states, "Thou shalt not kill," it includes the thought of preserving life—and not only our own life, but the lives of others. Some might have argued that Ahasuerus deserved to die. After all, he was a cruel man; therefore, they say, Mordecai should have remained silent. But he recognised his responsibility to the law of God. The same was true in regard to Esther; he had a duty to help her. (b) He served even though he served alone. Mordecai had no one to encourage him. He did not wait on others. (c) He served consistently and wisely (v. 11) every day, and even when the wicked king was involved.

Christian, God has you in a certain place, and He wants you to serve Him there. As C.H. Spurgeon said,

> Every child of God is where God has placed him for some purpose. You have been wishing for another position where you could do something for Jesus; do not wish anything of the kind, but serve him where you are. If you are sitting at the king's gate there is something for you to do there, and if you were on the queen's throne, there would be something for you to do there; do not ask to be either gatekeeper or queen, but whichever you are serve God therein. Mordecai did well because he acted as Mordecai should.[3]

How true. Do not imagine there is nothing for you to do. Your circumstances may not be what you want, but in the providence of God you are where you are. Therefore, serve Him as best you can.

GOD WILL NOT FORGET THE FAITHFUL SERVICE OF HIS PEOPLE.

According to Esther 2:23, Ahasuerus did not reward Mordecai immediately. However, his work was recorded and then rewarded in God's time! That reminds us of Hebrews 6:10: "For God is not unrighteous to forget your work and labour of love, which ye have shewed toward his name, in that ye have ministered to the saints, and do minister." It may seem that no one notices or cares

3   The Preacher's Homiletic Commentary: Notes derived from *Charles Haddon Spurgeon's Sermons on Women of the Bible*, 154, https://books.google.com/books?isbn=1598562843

or sees or remembers. But God does, and He will honour those who honour Him: at home, at work, in the church—wherever—and He will say, "Well done thou good and faithful servant." He is the rewarder of His people.

I see Mordecai revealing something of Christ. He was a despised man but he was faithful in his work and was rewarded. Christ was despised and rejected of men, but He was faithful in His redemptive work. He shall see the travail of His soul and be satisfied.

Let us learn from this man. God has placed us in our several places. We may not think there is much we can do. Our position in life may seem obscure and insignificant, or we may be in a position of authority and leadership—but wherever God has placed us, He had done so because He has something for us to do there. There is always work to do for God, at home, in society and in the church of Christ. Christian, serve Him fervently and faithfully, and be assured that He will not forget your labour of love.

4

Dealing with the Hamans of this World

After these things did king Ahasuerus promote Haman
the son of Hammedatha the Agagite, and advanced him,
and set his seat above all the princes that were with him.

Esther 3:1

Life in the Persian Empire during the reign of Ahasuerus was
full of intrigue, deception, betrayal, and revenge. This spirit
of ungodliness and rampant wickedness stretched from the highest offices in the land down to the common servant. There was
no moral foundation, resulting in a lot of unethical behaviour.
It seemed that every man did that which was right in his own
eyes. People lived by their own laws. Decisions were taken without reference to sound judgment. There was little or no sense of
accountability.

Given those circumstances, it is no surprise that we read of a
culture of drunkenness, divorce, immorality, and murder. Persia
was not a godly place. It was an empire where spiritual values

were hard to find and where life was cheap.

That truth comes to the fore in the final verses of Esther 2. These words describe a conspiracy against King Ahasuerus which involved two of his own men. However, these were not just any two men in the kingdom. Bigthan and Teresh were prominent figures in the empire. The word "chamberlains" in v. 21 refers to eunuchs who were appointed as ministers of state. When v. 21 states that they "kept the door," the words point to the fact that they were specially appointed guards who were charged with keeping or securing the king's sleeping area. This was a very trusted position. These men were responsible to keep the king safe when he was at his most vulnerable. They would have known the king's movements and the inside story on palace life. Most likely, the king appointed these men personally, and he relied upon their loyalty, bravery, and honesty. In one sense, he put his life into their hands.

Yet, it was these very men who were conspiring to put the king to death. It might be that certain commentators are right when they suggest that Bigthan and Teresh were planning to poison the king because he had married Esther—and that she was likely to be killed also. Or it might be that others are right when they suggest that they were going to behead him, then carry his severed head to Greece and present it as a trophy to their king. Be that as it may, the king was about to be betrayed by those of his own inner circle.

Before we go any further, there are certain things that are worth mentioning from this incident:

Firstly, sinful man is capable of any sin. The Old Testament tells us that the heart of man is deceitful above all things and desperately wicked, while the New Testament tells us that out of the heart proceed evil thoughts, murders, adulteries, fornications, thefts, false witness, blasphemies. If we needed proof of that, we have it here. This plan to murder the king came from the sinful hearts of these men. There is no sin the sinner is not capable of committing. These were trusted men, but they were full of betrayal, dishonesty, and murder. This is the outworking of sin, and there is no telling what any sinner will do.

Secondly, no sin stands alone. Verse 21 says, "they were wroth."

We are not told why that was the case, but it is enough for us to know that something happened that filled these men with great anger. The word "wroth" means to burst out with rage. The root of the word means to crack off; in other words, they were so enraged that they were ready to explode. Whatever had happened was serious enough in their minds to fill them with anger. It is interesting to note that these men were following the example set by their king. Remember the words of Esther 1:12? When Vashti refused to obey the king's command to come to his feast, we are told that he was "very wroth and his anger burned in him." It is the same word that is found in Esther 2:21. These men were about to burst with rage and were thinking of murdering the king. They were out of control. One sin gave way to another. They were on a downward course. Sin is like that; it rarely stands alone. Let anger go unchecked, and murder fills the heart; let lust go unchecked, and immorality will follow; let covetousness go unchecked, and there will be a huge temptation to steal or gamble or despise another person. Sin never stands by itself and it did not with these men.

Thirdly, the end of sin is death. The plan that these two men were hatching was never put into practice, for their conspiracy was revealed to the king by Mordecai the Jew. When the king found that his report was true, they were both hanged on a tree. It reminds me of the words of James 1:14, 15: "But every man is tempted, when he is drawn away of his own lust, and enticed. Then when lust hath conceived, it bringeth forth sin: and sin, when it is finished, bringeth forth death." Their sin was found out, and the upshot was that they lost their lives. The wages of sin may not always appear this way on earth; but remember, the wages of sin is death.

The plot to kill king Ahasuerus was foiled because of the truthful and timely actions of Mordecai the Jew. Had he not become aware of the conspiracy, and had he not believed it was true, and had he not then told Esther (who in turn was able to tell the king), then in all likelihood the king would have been killed. But in the providence of God, Mordecai did become aware of it, and he did what he had to do. That is how Esther 2 finishes. But Esther 3 opens with the tables turned, for in the opening verses of this chapter, we discover Mordecai being viewed as the villain—despised, hated, and facing death.

It is at this point that we are introduced to Haman. We are not long into this chapter before we realise that Haman's presence in the royal court leads to a very real and pressing crisis for the Jews. Things move quickly in this chapter. Ahasuerus makes reckless and thoughtless decisions; Haman uses his influence for the worst possible ends; Mordecai finds himself in the midst of a deep and dangerous controversy; and the future of the Jews is placed in the greatest jeopardy. Storm clouds are quickly gathering for God's people. It is important that we pause and consider Haman, Mordecai's reaction to him, and the crisis that follows— for, in a sense, what Mordecai faced is what God's people face and will face in a greater way in the future.

EVIL MEN OFTEN OCCUPY SIGNIFICANT POSITIONS.

When Mordecai reported the threat to the king's life (and thus was instrumental in saving his life, as described in the closing verses of Esther 2), we might have thought that he would receive immediate recognition and reward from the king. After all, he had shown himself to be a loyal servant, a faithful citizen, and an honest subject—things that were hard to find in Persia. But there was no immediate reward for Mordecai. The only reference is that his intervention was recorded in the book of the chronicles. That became very important later on, but for now there was no recognition, no appreciation, and no promotion. In fact, instead of Mordecai being promoted, Esther 3 opens with the promotion of the infamous Haman.

Notice carefully the words of v 1: "After these things did king Ahasuerus promote Haman the son of Hammedatha the Agagite, and advanced him, and set his seat above all the princes that were with him." Note those three phrases: (a) "Promote" means to honour. It carries the idea of making large, exalting, lifting up or magnifying; (b) "Advanced"— meaning, in the sense of honouring him, he lifted him or held him up high; and (c) "Set his seat above all the princes"—that is, he made a throne for him. These were the actions of Ahasuerus towards Haman. He gave him a position of prominence, of prestige, and of power.

This was another one of those reckless decisions by Ahasu-erus. I say that, because Haman was a proud, arrogant, self-cen-tred, cruel, and merciless man. He was not good for the king-dom. He was not an example of sound leadership. He was an impulsive man, a man who quickly allowed his emotions to run out of control. He was a man full of hatred, bitterness, anger, and resentment. Matthew Henry made the comment: "I wonder what the king saw in Haman that was commendable or meritori-ous; it is plain that he was not a man of honour or justice, of any true courage or steady conduct, but proud, and passionate, and revengeful; yet was he promoted, and caressed, and there was none so great as he." I have to wonder as well. Haman could well be described as Haman the Horrible! Yet, he was promoted. This evil man was now in a place of authority and influence.

Is that not often the way of the world? The ungodly seem to prosper. The sinful seem to get on in life. Ungodly men and wom-en end up in positions of power. Maybe you face that at work in an ungodly chief executive or manager, supervisor, or foreman. In some cases, the very highest offices in the land are occupied by godless people. Consider many of the kings who ruled over Isra-el; the majority of them were wicked people. Look at the officers who lived in the days of the disciples; wicked men like Herod were in power. Think of the days of the apostles; Nero was on the throne. Evil men were in prominent positions. Of course, the day will come when Antichrist will occupy a high office in the world, and people will follow him and bow themselves to worship him. We live in a world where wicked men are in high places. What are we to think of this?

The promotion of the wicked to high places is according to the purpose of God. God sets men up and God sets men down. Although these things are done on a human level—men pro-moting men, rulers being elected and elevated, presidents and prime-ministers winning the popular vote—behind it all is the hand of God. God overrules even this aspect of life. It was Jer-emiah who said, "Righteous art thou, O LORD, when I plead with thee: yet let me talk with thee of thy judgments: Wherefore doth the way of the wicked prosper? wherefore are all they happy that deal very treacherously? Thou hast planted them, yea, they have taken root: they grow, yea, they bring forth fruit:" (Jeremiah 12:1, 2) Note that, "thou hast planted him...." The wicked were prospering; they were in the place that God had planted them. The wicked are where they are in the sovereign purposes of God. He puts them where he wants them. Nebuchadnezzar is described as God's servant in Jeremiah 27:6. Think of that. Even the wicked are God's servants and do His will. They do not recognise that, but God orders it. Let us remember that when we see wicked men prosper. The bounds of their promotion and prosperity are set by God.

The promotion of the wicked to high places is temporary. Haman was exalted, but it was for a limited time. Their promotion does not mean that their sins are overlooked or that God turns a blind eye to their evil ways. Nor does it mean that they will be in that position of power and authority and prosperity for ever—not at all. God rules in the kingdoms of men, and kingdoms come and go, and rulers rise and fall at the Word of God. The wicked shall not always prosper. Their exaltation is limited.

The promotion of the wicked to high places often presents a test to God's people. Why does God order or allow this? Would it not be easier if godly men were in power? Would it not be better for the church of Christ if Christians were in positions of authority? Surely things would be better spiritually, morally, and socially if men of God were in charge? So why is it that wicked men get promoted over godly men? Part of the reason is for the sanctification of the church. If godly people were in power, we might be inclined to trust in them and not in God. As the Psalmist said, we are not to put our trust in princes nor in the sons of men with whom there is no help (Psalm 146:3). We are to put our trust in the Lord. And when wicked men are in power, we have more reason to do that than ever.

Psalm 75:7, 8 are timely words on this subject: "For promotion cometh neither from the east, nor from the west, nor from the south. But God is the judge: he putteth down one, and setteth up another." Let us not lose sight of that. God is the judge, and promotion comes from Him. We should remember these words in the confusion and chaos that surrounds the nations of the world in these days. Remember, He is the perfect judge. He does all things well at all times. He does all things for His own glory, and He performs all things for the good of His people. We might not see that right now, but let us trust in the loving and all-wise God whom we serve.

FAITHFULNESS TO GOD IS MORE IMPORTANT THAN OBEDIENCE TO MEN.

Verse 2 marks a tremendous contrast between Mordecai and the other officers who sat in the king's gate. Some might argue that until this point there was no visible difference between this Jew and the other men. They may allege that Mordecai lived in such a way that it was impossible to tell that he was one of God's covenant people, that he was weak and worldly, just like all those around him. I disagree with that assessment. When we come into Esther 3, we discover Mordecai standing firm, standing out and standing apart from all the others. Remember the context of these verses. Haman had been promoted by the king, with the command that all the king's servants would bow down and reverence him. All of them did—all except one. And this is where Mordecai comes to the fore, and where the great contrast appears. Verse 2 records, "All the king's servants that were in the king's gate bowed and reverenced Haman; for the king had so commanded concerning him. But Mordecai bowed not nor did him reverence." Mordecai defied the king's command. He refused to honour this wicked man. He preferred to be faithful to God, rather than obey the command of a pagan king. There are two things here:

THE REASON FOR MORDECAI'S ACTIONS

Why did he do this? Why did he refuse to bow before Haman? The answer to that question may lie in the words of v. 1 and v. 2. In v. 1, we are told that Haman was an Agagite—that is, he was a descendant of Agag who was Amalekite king in the days of Saul. Back in 1 Samuel 15, Saul refused to kill Agag despite the clear command of God and despite the fact that God had sworn in Exodus 17 to have war with the Amalekites from generation to generation. In other words, this man Haman was from a line of people who were the enemies of God. Therefore, Mordecai did not want to honour that which God had cursed.

Then, v. 2 tells us that the king's command had to do with bowing down and reverencing Haman. The words "bowed" and "reverenced" are strong terms and relate to the kind of honour reserved for God. Mordecai would not give that kind of honour to a man. This reverence that Haman expected was not a mere civic formality or a piece of public protocol. There was more to it; and as a Jew, Mordecai refused to comply. It is interesting to note that in chapter 1 he advised Esther not to reveal her Jewishness. But in chapter 3:4, he revealed his. Why? Because this issue of bowing before Haman was so serious, indeed, so huge, that he was now ready to declare that he was Jew. And because he was a Jew, he would have no part in this reverencing of Haman. His stand against Haman was because he wanted to obey the law of God.

THE RESOLVE IN MORDECAI'S ACTIONS

The other officers in the gate could not understand his refusal to bow, so they pressed him. Consider vv. 3, 4. They asked him every day, "Why do you do this? Why do you break the king's command? Why will you not do as you are directed? Why not comply with the protocol? Why do you not do what everyone else is doing?" But every day he refused. As v. 4 puts it, "He hearkened not unto them." He heard them, but he would not heed their counsel. He did not allow his peers to pressure him into this kind of action.

There he was, the only one refusing to bow before this ungodly man. Matthew Henry said, "His refusal was pious, conscientious, and pleasing to God, for the religion of a Jew forbade him." He obeyed God rather than men.

We are in a day where standing for Christ is frowned upon, even by some who profess to know Christ. It is a day where political correctness has swept into the church. The idea that standing against sin is unloving has silenced many believers. There is a fear of saying you are against something in case you might be labelled a bigot, legalist or being harsh. In that kind of atmosphere, all kinds of sins flourish.

The Christian is called to take a stand against false doctrine and to stand against idolatry; he is called to have no fellowship with the unfruitful works of darkness and to separate himself from apostasy; he is called to live differently from the world and to oppose the works of darkness and the ways of hell. And he is called to test or try the spirits, to discern between right and wrong—called to resist the devil. So it is not unloving to be faithful to God, even though that puts us at odds with the world.

I fear we are losing that spirit of resistance to the ways of the world. The Christian who is not willing to stand up for Christ in any circumstance gives little evidence of true love to Christ. Where God's honour is at stake, we have no option but to obey God rather than men. This is how Christians have lived their lives in the past. The Apostles, the Reformers, the Puritans were all of this mind: "I will obey God at any cost, even the loss of my life." Where is that spirit today?

OBEDIENCE TO GOD WILL INCITE THE WORLD'S HATRED AGAINST GOD'S PEOPLE.

It would be a terrible understatement to suggest that Haman was displeased with Mordecai's actions towards him. The refusal of the Jew to bow before him was more than Haman could bear. He was not slighty grieved; he was completely enraged. Esther 3:5 records "...when Haman saw that Mordecai bowed not, nor did him reverence, then was Haman full of wrath." The "when" and "then" of this verse are important as they suggest that Haman's anger was both immediate and intense. He was thoroughly intolerant of any perceived disrespect shown to him. Although others bowed before him and paid him reverence, the fact the one man—Mordecai—refused to do so was a huge fly in the ointment. Haman could not conceal his anger. Such was his anger that he began to formulate the idea of putting the Jews to death. The language of v. 6, and especially the words, "he thought scorn to lay hands on Mordecai" reveal that Haman was not prepared to suffer this insult quietly.

His mind went into overdrive and his heart was full of hatred.

It is clear from all that is said in these verses (and we will return to the plan to destroy the Jews in a later chapter), that there was a great conflict in place. A battle was raging. Haman was full of animosity towards a man who sought to obey God's law.

This truth brings us back to the Garden of Eden and to the words of Genesis 3:15 where God promised the Serpent, "And I will put enmity between thee and the woman, and between thy seed and her seed; it shall bruise thy head, and thou shalt bruise his heel." Ever since that time, the world, the flesh, and the devil have opposed the things and people of God. This is the battle that still rages today. Which side are you on?

5

If God Be for Us

In the first month, that is, the month Nisan, in the
twelfth year of king Ahasuerus, they cast Pur, that is, the
lot, before Haman from day to day, and from month to
month, to the twelfth month, that is, the month Adar.

Esther 3:7

The first two chapters of the book of Esther record a time of great change, turmoil, and commotion within the Persian Empire. When the book opens, Ahasuerus (the king of Persia) was in the middle of a prolonged feast with the princes, servants, officers, and advisors of his kingdom. It was no ordinary feast, but a prolonged affair of drinking, talking, and planning. At the centre of their thoughts was a plan to fight against Greece and bring it under Persian authority. The days and weeks were filled with typical Persian behaviour. Drunkenness was common. The king was quick to boast of his riches, and there was a proud air of expectancy that the war would be swift and the victory sure. The idea of defeat would not have featured much in their thinking.

But unknown to Ahasuerus, he was going to face huge problems on two very different fronts. One was from his wife. In the midst of that drunken feast, the king called Vashti to appear before him while he sat with the other men. It was an absurd request. She flatly refused it, and as a result he flew into a rage. Esther 1:12 records that, "he was very wroth and his anger burned within him." To use modern language, "He lost it!" He felt grossly and publicly insulted, and when he consulted with his servants—his lawyers—they advised him for the sake of all the men of the kingdom to put her away. Ahasuerus acted on that advice, and before chapter 1 finishes, their marriage was over. It was a time of great personal turmoil for him. He lost his wife.

He also lost the war. Historians record that the Persian campaign against Greece did not end in victory; therefore, the king returned to the empty palace a defeated man. That is why I say these opening chapters record a time of great change, turmoil, and commotion within the Persian Empire.

It was at this time (four or five years after he had divorced Vashti), that Ahasuerus took Esther as his wife. It seems for the next four or five years, things were relatively calm and quiet in the kingdom.

All that was about to change. When chapter 2 closes, Ahasuerus was on the throne; Esther was the queen; Mordecai (a Jew) was sitting in the king's gate, and his faithfulness to the king had been recorded. We might well wonder what could go wrong for the Jews living in Persia. What problems were they likely to face? How could things start to unravel for them? However, that is exactly what happened in chapter 3, and much of this focuses on a man called Haman. In v. 1 we are given important information concerning his background. His father was Hammedatha who was an Agagite, and that links him to the Amalekites (Agag was an Amalekite king referred to in 1 Samuel 15). We know from Exodus 17 that there was a bitter war between the Israelites and Amalekites in the days of Moses. There was an ongoing conflict between these two nations.

Therefore, this man did not come from a people who were friendly towards the people of God. His family line was full of

hatred for the Jews. In chapter 3, Haman was suddenly and inex-
plicably promoted to a very high position in the land. The terms
of his promotion meant that the other officers were to bow down
to him. He was given a position of authority above all the princes
that were before him. The members or officers of the royal court
were expected to give the equivalent of religious honour to Haman. I can only imagine the sense of pride that would have filled
his heart. He was the king's favourite. He was pre-eminent. All
eyes were on him. It would have been impossible to be in the vi-
cinity of the palace and not notice when Haman walked past, for
the other men had to respond in this humiliating way. Haman
the Agagite was the special one.

However, there was a fly in the ointment—one man who was
not prepared to worship this proud Persian. As Esther 3:2 records,
"Mordecai bowed not nor did him reverence." Haman was aware
of that; and when he learned that he was Jew, Haman began to
burn with rage. He took Mordecai's refusal to reverence him as
a personal insult. He saw it as an act of contempt. He hated him
for it. And at this point a fire was beginning to burn that had the
potential to wipe out all the Jews in the kingdom of Persia. Consider the language of Esther 3:5, 6: "And when Haman saw that
Mordecai bowed not, nor did him reverence, then was Haman
full of wrath. And he thought scorn to lay hands on Mordecai
alone; for they had shewed him the people of Mordecai: wherefore Haman sought to destroy all the Jews that were throughout
the whole kingdom of Ahasuerus, even the people of Mordecai."
Notice that; he thought scorn (in other words he thought it con-
temptible to deal with Mordecai alone), so he widened his net
and sought to destroy all of the Jews.

Pay attention to the sequence of events. Haman's pride led
to anger and his anger led to ideas of murder. There is no telling
where human pride will lead to. Pride makes a man think he can
live above God, live against God, and live without God. It will
make him think that he has the right to do as he pleases. It will
lead him on a course of other sins. It will mean he thinks he is
always right and that his opinions are supreme. He will believe
that he is lord of all and that none can challenge him or condemn
him. Pride makes a man live like the devil and makes him feel

secure in his own little, vain world. Haman was like that. He was proud, and when Mordecai did not comply with his status, the evil intents of his heart were made known.

In one sense Haman stands in the forefront of this chapter. But as we have come to see in the book of Esther, God is behind the scenes. God's people were facing a huge threat; however, while man was against them, God was for them. And that has to be an encouraging truth for God's people in this age. These last days are perilous times. There is trouble brewing and breaking on so many fronts against the church of Christ. Believers are being persecuted; the gospel is under attack; Christianity is being undermined; and Satan is busy and problems are appearing. In the midst of it all, let us never forget that God is for us. I have two major thoughts as we consider this theme:

THE UNVEILING OF A WICKED PLAN AGAINST GOD'S PEOPLE

Haman is described in Esther 3:10 as the "Jews' enemy." The word "enemy" could be translated by the word oppressor or the word adversary. In fact, the Hebrew word comes from a term that means to cramp or to trouble or to vex. In other words, Haman was ready to move against the Jews and execute a wicked and evil plan against them. As he looked at Mordecai refusing to bow down before him, he began to formulate in his mind a way of striking back. He became consumed with this. It occupied his thoughts every day. That is why v. 6 opens with the words: "And he thought...." He deliberated as to the best way forward. Should he just go after Mordecai? Should he just take revenge on him or should he go further and get rid of all the Jews at one time? So, as time passed he made plans. Then, in v. 8, he went into king Ahasuerus and unveiled his plan before him.

Why is this important for us? Why should we consider this? Because we need to understand that as God's people we are in a similar situation. What was happening in Persia can be traced right back to Genesis 3:15 where God said to Satan, "And I will put enmity between thee and the woman, and between thy seed and her seed; it shall bruise thy head, and thou shalt bruise his heel." There is a conflict between Christ and Satan. And those who are Christ's, that is, those who are in union with Christ, are in the midst of this fight. The world is not friendly towards God or His people. This present evil world (as Paul calls it in Galatians 1) is at odds with righteousness and holiness. The difference is like day and night. On one hand, there is the truth of the gospel and all that pertains to godliness, whereas on the other hand there is sin and lust and worldliness. In Ephesians 6, Paul spoke of principalities and powers and rulers of the darkness of this world and spiritual wickedness in high places. And then he urged the Christians to "withstand in the evil day." Paul told Timothy to "fight the good fight of faith" and to "endure hardness as a good soldier of Jesus Christ." There is a mighty conflict going on. Satan and his servants have plans against the church of Christ.

This is no new thing. The history of the people of God has been a history of trouble and oppression as evil men seek to bring the church of Christ into ruin. In the Old Testament it was the Amalekites, Midianites, and Philistines. While the names have changed and circumstances are different, the battle goes on, and it will go on. Then the final great enemy of God's people will appear. Antichrist will step on the stage of world affairs. And what will he do? He will fight against God's people. (Incidentally, Haman prefigures Antichrist—not just in his rise and power, but also in his fall and destruction.) Let us not dismiss this historical account, thinking it is not relevant for us. It is highly relevant. Therefore, we should pay particular attention to it. Look at the details of this and note the following points.

THE ACCUSATION IN HIS PLAN

When Haman stood before the king, he accused the Jews in Persia of being rebels. Consider the exact wording in v. 8 and note that he could not even bring himself to call them Jews. He scathingly called them "a certain people," and then he went on to accuse them of crimes against the king. He alleged that their laws were different and that the people did not keep the king's laws. There was no evidence of that except that Mordecai did not bow down to him. The Jews were a law-abiding people. The Persians had nothing to fear from them. They were not set on rebelling; they were living peaceably throughout the kingdom. But he made a malicious accusation against them. Is that not how the devil works? He deals in half-truths; he is a liar from the beginning; he misrepresents God's people; he is not interested in the whole truth. Those who oppose the church of Christ are happy to bend the facts to suit their own ends. They accuse us of being against the good of society, of being fanatics—bigots—while all the time, God's people are the salt of the earth.

THE AIM OF HIS PLAN

This is mentioned in vv. 6, 9, and 13. It was his intention to destroy the Jews. The Hebrew word translated "destroy" means to overthrow or bring to utter desolation. He did not want one of them to remain. According to v. 13, he wanted them to be destroyed, to be killed, and to perish. Not just some of them, but all of them— young and old, little children and women—all of them in one day. That has ever been Satan's plan. There is history here. Cain killed Abel. Pharaoh tried to wipe out the Hebrews in Egypt. Herod tried to destroy them in the days of Christ. Satan despises the people of God. He hates Christ, and he would persecute the church of Christ to death if he could. And he will continue with that aim. Anything Christian, even nominally Christian, is under attack.

THE ARGUMENT IN HIS PLAN

Consider v. 9 and note how Haman was thinking ahead. He reasoned that the king might not be happy if he was no longer receiving revenue from the Jews. So, Haman promised him that he would take care of that. He would pay into the king's treasury. It was a huge sum of money. In today's terms it would run into millions or even billions of pounds or dollars. Haman was essentially saying there would be no loss to the kingdom. "King, you have nothing to lose." They say money talks, and it talked here.

THE APPROVAL OF HIS PLAN

Ahasuerus listened to Haman as he presented this proposal. Then he took his ring off and gave it to Haman. With the king's ring, he was able to sign, seal, and deliver the instructions and thus put his plan into operation. The king approved it. There is a very solemn lesson here for all of us. The king made a decision without due care and consideration. He did not make enquiry as to the accuracy of Haman's word. He did not ask counsel from others. He did not search the books for precedents or directions. He listened to one man and, on the basis of that man's word, he consented to the slaughter of the Jews. It is no wonder Proverbs 24:6 states, "in multitude of counsellors there is safety." Ahasuerus made a terrible decision without proper thought.

THE ADVANCING OF HIS PLAN

Note the speed with which Haman put this evil scheme in place: vv. 12-15 mention that "the posts went out being hastened by the king's commandment." Haman could almost smell blood by now, and he wanted to waste no time in what he was planning to do. He could not wait to be rid of the Jews from the land.

There is no question that this was an evil plan against God's people. Haman was stirred against them, and he succeeded in stirring others against them too. His anger gave way to murder, and he set this plan in motion to deal with God's people once and for all. The Jews were facing complete destruction. Let us understand this: we are in a world that displays the very same hatred towards the people of God. Christian people are persecuted; Christian values are ignored; Christian businesses have been pursued in the courts; and Christian witness is almost drowned out by an unbelieving and uncaring world. However, what we see now is nothing in comparison with what will happen in the future. Scripture speaks of a time of tribulation. Revelation 13 details the rise of Antichrist and the fact that with his armies and forces he will make war with the saints. Satan is intent on destroying the people of God.

It happens on a personal level, also. Remember what Christ said to Peter and the other disciples in Luke 22:31: "Satan has desired to have you to sift you as wheat." He is the wicked adversary of God's people, the one who walks about like a roaring lion seeking whom he may devour. We are in a battle—a spiritual warfare, a struggle with the powers of darkness. Haman may be dead, but the plans he had for God's covenant people have a modern-day counterpart: the unveiling of a wicked plan against God's people.

THE OVERRULING BY A WONDERFUL PROVIDENCE FOR GOD'S PEOPLE.

When the idea came to Haman to destroy the Jews, one of the first things he considered was the timing of the massacre. In order to determine that, he turned to the established practice of casting lots. Verse 7 records, "In the first month, that is, the month Nisan, in the twelfth year of king Ahasuerus, they cast Pur, that is, the lot, before Haman from day to day, and from month to month, to the twelfth month, that is, the month Adar." It seems that he cast the lot to determine which month would be the best to move against the Jews. Then he cast the lot again to determine which day of that month would be best. As a result of that process, the date was set (according to v. 13) for the thirteenth day of the twelfth month. That meant Haman's plan was set to be executed in eleven months' time.

Haman followed the common practice of throwing lots, and the lot set the date months in the future. Why is that important? It is important because it gave Esther and Mordecai the opportunity to act against this plan and move in order to see the Jews spared. Had the lot given a date just a few days ahead, there would have been little or nothing they could have done. As it was, they were given the necessary time. To the outsider that looks to be accidental—just the luck of the dice or the luck of the draw. As believers we know differently, for in Proverbs 16:33 we read, "The lot is cast into the lap; but the whole disposing thereof is of the LORD." What does that mean? It means that while man does what he does, God overrules it all. Matthew Henry noted, "Nothing comes to pass by chance, nor is an event determined by a blind fortune, but everything by the will and counsel of God." Charles Bridges in his commentary on Proverbs notes, "The instructive lesson to learn is that there is no blank in the most minute circumstances. Everything is a wheel of providence. Who can fail to see the hand of God, most wonderful in the most apparently casual contingencies, overruling all second causes to fulfill his will, while they work their own way. Not one event can fly out of the bounds of providence." Proverbs 16:9 underscores that truth when it says, "A man's heart deviseth his way: but the LORD directeth his steps." We see this again and again in this book. God is in control. It is interesting to note that in v. 1 we read that Ahasuerus promoted Haman and set his seat above all the princes that were with him. The word "seat" means a throne. Haman was in a position of high authority in Persia. He acted like the king. He thought he was greater than the king. However, he failed to understand that there was a higher throne than his, a greater King, a great Judge, a greater Ruler than he. There is One who rules and reigns in the kingdoms of men. His throne is in the heavens and none can overthrow, overrule or overcome Him. Haman thought he was invincible; but he failed to consider the infinite and eternal and unchangeable God of heaven. This eleven-month space gave time for deliverance to come. Haman was overruled by a wonderful—and, right now, an unseen—providence. How good is the God we adore!

There is one further observation here, by way of contrast, an observation that relates to God's people personally. Haman was an evil enemy of God's people; he was in every sense their adversary. When he brought an accusation against Mordecai and God's people, Ahasuerus sided with him. He approved it and set his seal upon it. Therefore, at that point, the Jews had no one to plead for them.

It is different for the Christian. When Satan comes as our adversary to accuse us, to stand against us and to resist us, we have an advocate in Christ. Christ pleads our case and presents His blood before the Father' throne. We are justified in Him, and what does that mean? It means God is for us. As believers we cannot be condemned, for Christ has already borne that condemnation. Our sin is gone, never to be remembered against us again. Our God and Saviour has removed it as far as the east is from the west. We are washed and accepted as holy and righteous in his sight. Therefore, we can say, "Who is he that condemneth? It is Christ who died, rose again, who ascended to glory, who is seated at the Father's right hand and who ever lives to pray for His people." Our God is on the throne. Take heart, if you are a believer. All is well—now and for ever.

6

For Such a Time as This

For if thou altogether holdest thy peace at this time, then shall there enlargement and deliverance arise to the Jews from another place; but thou and thy father's house shall be destroyed: and who knoweth whether thou art come to the kingdom for such a time as this?

Esther 4:14

Of the five main characters that feature in the book of Esther there is nothing good that can be said about Haman the Agagite. When he first appears in Esther 3, he is portrayed as a proud, self-centred, arrogant, and extremely malicious kind of man. By the decree of the king, as we have already noted, he had become a prominent figure in the royal court and occupied a very powerful position in the Persian government. Other officers were commanded to bow down to him and he expected and enjoyed their homage.

As far as position and prestige were concerned, Haman had it all. He was a very wealthy man and loved the pre-eminence that he had gained in the nation. If he were alive today, he would be constantly in the news—bragging and boasting of his achievements—and looking to be honoured at every opportunity. And yet for all of that, Haman was intensely unhappy. The reason for his unhappiness centered on the fact that Mordecai, a Jew, refused to give him the respect that he felt he deserved. Mordecai would not bow down to him nor reverence him. To him it would have been an act of idolatry, and God's law prohibited any such worship to men. There was no love lost between these two men.

We might think that Haman could have put such a thing to the back of his mind. After all, everyone else worshipped him, and his position in the kingdom seemed secure. But such was his pride and arrogance that Mordecai's actions filled him with anger—so much so that he went to the king and succeeded in having a law passed that sentenced—not just Mordecai—but all the Jews in the kingdom—to death. His plan was one of genocide. Not one Jew—young or old, man or woman—was to be spared. They had been in Persia for several generations by this time—and had posed no threat to the king or his Empire, but he wanted to destroy them in one day.

When that law was passed and announced throughout the 127 provinces of the kingdom, there were two very different reactions. On one hand, Haman and the king sat down to drink wine. There was a sense of self-satisfaction. Haman thought the deed was as good as done. He could sit back, relax, and wait for the planned day to arrive. He was confident that there would be no slip ups, no problems, no obstacles. After all, this massacre was now enshrined in Persian law. What could go wrong? It was time for a drink.

But while he and the king sat at ease, the Jews throughout the kingdom were in a state of utter disbelief and consternation. That is how Esther 4 opens: "When Mordecai perceived all that was done..." In other words, when he heard the contents of the king's letter; when he realised that a date had been set; when he understood that all of his people were going to be massacred throughout the kingdom; when he perceived all that was done, "he rent his clothes, and put on sackcloth and ashes and went out into the streets of the city and cried with a loud and bitter cry." Remember, Mordecai was no ordinary member of the public. He was an officer in the royal court. He was one of the government officials. But there he was—in the middle of the city of Shushan—weeping and wailing and mourning over what was being planned against him and his people. There can be no doubt that he linked this to Haman's hatred of him. Therefore, he would have felt this more keenly than most. It was one thing for his life to be in danger; he was ready for that—but it was another thing for the entire Jewish population to be facing death. Mordecai was distraught. And how he reacted was exactly how other Jews reacted.

The Jewish population of Persia was in an uproar. The king's command had come unexpectedly, and since it was the law of the king it was considered to be unchangeable. Put yourself in their position. They appeared to be just months away from complete destruction, and they were powerless. The Jews mourned, wept, and fasted and put on sackcloth and ashes.

At last, Esther heard about Mordecai. As she had no idea what had happened, she sent clothes out to him so that he could change out of his sackcloth; but he promptly returned them. Then she sent one of her servants out to ask the reason for the weeping and mourning. On this occasion, Mordecai sent her a copy of the king's letter and a message that she must go into the king and plead with him to spare her people. When Esther heard that, she knew what it meant.

It meant almost certain death for her. For as she explained to Mordecai through her servant, it was Persian law that no one could approach the king unless he asked for such a person to come. To breach that protocol would result in death, and the king had not asked for her for thirty days. It is as if Esther was saying, "I have no way into the king. I have no access to him. I cannot approach him, and if I do, I will die...." Then Mordecai sent an answer back in which he firmly and passionately said to his adopted daughter, and I paraphrase, "Esther—do not think that you will escape this massacre. If you do nothing or say nothing, deliverance will arise to the Jews from somewhere else, but you and your family will perish. But who knows, whether you have come to the kingdom for such a time as this."

Mordecai was not speaking in generalities. He was pressing home the solemn personal responsibility that was now upon Esther. She needed to act. Mordecai was not being over dramatic. He was not scaremongering. It really was a life-or-death situation, not just for her, but for all of the Jews living throughout the kingdom. He was reminding her that in the providence of God, she had been placed in this position for a reason, and now it was time to step up and do what God had put her in the palace to do. It was an impassioned plea for her to approach the king on behalf of her people and thus seek to secure their deliverance. "And who knoweth whether thou art come to the kingdom for such a time as this?"

These words have become one of the most memorable statements of the book. Let us leave Esther aside for a moment, for these words have a message for every one of God's people. This is something we must consider very carefully—and I use the word *consider* intentionally. In v. 13, Mordecai said to his cousin, "think not..." and then in v. 14 he said, "who knoweth whether thou art come to the kingdom for such a time as this...." In other words, he is saying to her: "Do not think this way, but consider this: who knows, who call tell, but this is God's will for you." He wanted her to consider certain things, and there are certain things that we need to consider also. This is not just a page from history. This has a very important message for us. These things have been written for our learning; therefore, we must consider what God would teach us. To put it simply, we are here for such a time as this. With that in mind, consider these three truths:

GOD HAS A WORK FOR HIS PEOPLE TO DO IN EVIL TIMES.

We hardly need to be reminded that these words were first spoken by Mordecai in a time of great crisis for God's people. Their entire future was in jeopardy. Their families were about to be torn apart: mothers and fathers were going to die; children were going to be destroyed; their whole way of life was going to be extinguished from the kingdom. Haman, that bitter adversary of the Jews, was in the wings just waiting to execute his wicked plan against God's people. It was therefore an extremely evil time in their history. They were about to be destroyed. That is the context of the phrase "such a time as this." There was little to encourage, little to hearten, little to cheer the Jews.

Nevertheless, it was right at this time that Esther was being urged to do something. Consider the language of v. 8 and v. 14. Mordecai charged Esther that she should go in to the king to plead before him for her people. According to v. 14, she was not to hold her peace. That is, she was not to remain silent or still. Esther's duty was clear. She needed to go into the king, identify herself as a Jew, expose the sin and wickedness of Haman, plead for the salvation of her people, and endeavour to overthrow and overturn the law that had been signed. To put it simply, Esther was being asked to take a stand for God and His covenant people.

Is there not a parallel for God's people in this day? There is a work that we are called to do for God. Is it not our responsibility to stand up for Christ amid all of the wickedness and sinfulness of this age? Is it not our responsibility to expose every plan to destroy Christ's church? Is it not our responsibility to do all we can to see our children saved from the evil plans of Satan? Is it not our duty to strive for the salvation of those outside our family who are in danger of eternal death? It is not our responsibility to speak a word in season to a lost and dying world? Is it not our responsibility to be the salt of the earth and the light of the world? Is it not our responsibility to serve our God and to be faithful to Him? Are we not charged by gospel precepts to be distinct from the world and have no fellowship with the unfruitful works of darkness? Are we not charged to unashamedly identify with the saints and declare by our words and our actions that we are on the Lord's side? This is the message of this passage: God has a work for His people to do in evil times. Note:

THIS WORK IS THE PERSONAL RESPONSIBILITY OF EVERY CHRISTIAN.

Mordecai was speaking directly to Esther, and as he did, he stressed her personal responsibility. Notice how that is emphasised in vv. 13, 14: "Thou art come." In fact, the force of these words stresses that this was something only Esther could do. Others had their duty, but this was hers. We, too, have a personal responsibility to stand for God. We sometimes say this is the work of the church—but Christians *are* the church!

THIS WORK IS EXTREMELY PRESSING AND URGENT.

It is impossible to read the words of Mordecai's message and not detect the urgency that he was calling for. Time was short for the Jews. The black thunderous clouds of trouble were casting a very dark shadow over the Lord's people. Evil men were busy at work. Plans were being finalised. Schemes were being put into place even as Mordecai was speaking. There was no time to waste. Likewise, we have no time to waste in being faithful to God.

THIS WORK IS BESET WITH DANGERS AND TROUBLES.

Esther could die! It could cost her everything she had. This is clear from v. 11. She would have to risk life and limb to go into the king. Her work was not at all easy. Following Christ can be costly. There is a price to pay for being faithful to the Lord Jesus. We can lose friends, promotions at work, and the acclaim of men. We can find ourselves isolated and forsaken. In some cases, Christians lose far more; they lose their lives. However, there is still a work to be done.

THIS WORK HAS IMPORTANT RAMIFICATIONS FOR THE FUTURE.

What Esther was being called to do would impact generations to come. It was not just about her; it was about children and children's children.

I see a very clear parallel in our time. These are evil days. The enemy of God's people is busy. Satan has come in like a flood against the church. He is set on our destruction. Our children are under serious threat from a world that cares nothing for their souls. Therefore, it is time to recognise that we have work to do. Do we sense that? Are we not aware that there is gospel work we are called to engage in? The Christian is not saved *by* his works, but he is saved *unto* good works (Ephesians 2:8-10). We are servants of God, and there is a mammoth work for us to do.

The Psalmist spoke of a time for God to work. This is also a time for us to work. And one of the greatest things we can do is presented by contrast here. Esther was being urged to go into the king and plead for her people. She did not have ready access because he had not invited her. We are invited to plead before the King of heaven for His people, His church, and we do have access to the throne, through our Lord Jesus Christ. This is not only something we *can* do; it is something we *must* do. God has a work for His people to do in evil times.

GOD APPOINTS AND PREPARES HIS PEOPLE FOR THIS WORK.

Mordecai did not merely set this great challenge before Esther. He also presented her with a compelling argument. Notice the words of v. 14: "Who knoweth whether thou art come to the kingdom for such a time as this." What did he mean by that? What was he really saying? He was asking Esther to consider the truth that God had placed her in the palace so that she would be in the right place at the right time to intervene on behalf of His people.

This was a call for Esther to look back and to ponder all that had happened in her life. Then, she was to realise that all those events—all those experiences, all those upheavals, all those trials, all those changes, all those seemingly strange providences—were all of God and were meticulously designed for this purpose: that she might be the means of doing this great work for Him and His people.

In other words, God had prepared her and placed her in the palace for a reason. Think of what was involved in all of that. She was still living in Persia when other Jews had returned home. The beauty God had given her meant that she was chosen to appear before the king. Due to her supreme character and appearance she was made queen. She had wisdom to obey her cousin and not reveal her Jewish background at an earlier time, and she found favour with the king. For a number of years, she lived without major incident in the palace.

None of these things was by accident. Esther was where she was because God wanted her there. I understand the wickedness of the King's court and the extremely unconventional events in the earlier chapters. There were many unusual or unsavoury things as far as the king was concerned. But God was working all things together for the good of his people. This was all by divine appointment. Esther's placement in the palace, Esther's preparation in the palace, and Esther's preferment in the palace—none of that was coincidental. God wanted her there at this very time so that she could be the means of serving Him and His people. What a lesson in God's perfect providence. Think of that—and consider how personal, precise, purposeful, and prevailing God's providence is in the lives of His people. If one step had failed along the way, Esther would not have been where she was.

What do we learn from this? We surely learn that God has placed us where we are because He has something He wants us to do. C.H. Spurgeon asked, "Why are you placed where you are? Brother, your inevitable answer must be that God has put you where you are for some good purpose, which purpose must be connected with his own glory and with the extension of his kingdom in the world."[4] If I can put it this way, God has placed us in this world at this time to meet the challenge of this hour. This is not some vague observation or impractical truth.

Where are you right now in life? In school? God has something for you to do there. At home with children, and maybe feeling worthless and useless? You have a phenomenal opportunity to do good among your own children. In a place of work that is hard and difficult? You have come to that place for such a time as this.

Why were we not born in the days of the Reformation or in days of revival, or in days of the Great Awakenings? Why were we not born in Africa or India or Australia? Why did God save your soul and direct your steps this way? Why did He order it that you and I would live in days of deepening apostasy, compromise, and spiritual declension? Why did He appoint our circumstances as they are? Because in His sovereign purpose He has us brought to the kingdom for such a time as this. Let me make three observations with that in mind: (a) There is a reason God has placed us where He has. Otherwise, He would have placed us somewhere else. (b) We should strive to serve Him where we are. If God has placed us where we are, then His remarkable dealings with us compel us to serve Him where He has placed us. (c) There is a

4   Charles Haddon Spurgeon, *The Complete Works of C. H. Spurgeon, Volume 30*: Sermons 1757-1815, Sermon 1778: *Esther's Exaltation, or, Who Knoweth*, A Sermon Delivered on the Lord's Day Morning April 27th, 1884

true contentment in serving God where He has placed us. Better to be in the Persian court with all of its trials and troubles and be in God's will, than to be somewhere easier but be outside God's will.

I do not know your circumstances right now but I know this: God has not placed you where you are so that you can simply enjoy what He has given you and live the rest of your life for yourself. He has appointed your place for His service. Is this truth not clear from the life of Joseph? His brothers had meant things for evil but God had meant them for good. Joseph was in Egypt by divine appointment and God had a lifesaving work there for him to do. God makes no mistakes.

God has a work for His people to do in evil times and He appoints and prepares His people for that work.

God Graciously Encourages His People to Fulfil this Work for Him.

If Mordecai's statement was true—that Esther had come to the kingdom for such a time as this—and it was—then Esther had every reason to go forward. Verse 14 is not just an argument for action; it is an encouragement for action. God was with her. God had ordered these things. God was in control. Therefore, she could step out, be daring, and go to the king. These words are full of encouragement. Is that not just like the Lord? When God reveals His will for our lives and impresses upon us the sense of duty, He quickly follows it up with words of comfort and strength. He called Joshua to lead the people of Israel into the Promised Land and, at the same time, told him not to be dismayed but to be of good courage.

Is God calling you to a particular service for Him? Is He leading you along a hard and difficult course in life? Do not be discouraged. God knows what He is doing for you, in you, and with you.

Therefore, let us press on and say with Esther, "So will I go into the king." Press on, dear Christian. God has brought you to the kingdom for such a time as this. Be confident. Be courageous. Be content.

7

Faithful to God, Whatever the Cost

Then Esther bade them return Mordecai this answer, Go,
gather together all the Jews that are present in Shushan,
and fast ye for me, and neither eat nor drink three days,
night or day: I also and my maidens will fast likewise;
and so will I go in unto the king, which is not according
to the law: and if I perish, I perish.

Esther 4:15, 16

Esther chapter 4 records in no small detail the reaction of Mordecai and Esther to the plans that had been laid for the slaughter of the Jews throughout the Persian Empire.

When Haman, the Jews' enemy, succeeded in having the king sign his planned genocide into law, letters were immediately sent throughout the kingdom. Those letters contained all the necessary details: on the thirteenth day of the twelfth month, every Jew—man, woman, and child—was to be put to death. None was to escape. None was to be spared. The entire Jewish population in Persia were to be put to death and all their possessions were to be taken as a spoil of war.

When Mordecai the Jew heard of this devilish plot he understood exactly what it meant, and he reacted in a threefold way.

First there was consternation. Verse 1 records that "he rent his clothes, put on sackcloth and ashes, and went out into the midst of the city, and cried with a loud and bitter cry." None of these words is redundant. The tearing of his clothes signified the great and intense anguish that he felt. The rending of the garments was a sign of the most oppressive grief. He was distraught at what he had heard. Then he put on sackcloth and ashes. Sackcloth is first mentioned in Scripture in Genesis 37 in connection with Jacob mourning over his son Joseph, and it is often used to highlight the distress that comes with the death of a loved one. When Mordecai put on sackcloth and ashes it was to express the horror of what the Jews were facing. Then he went out into the city and wept and wailed with a loud and bitter cry. Mordecai was a distinguished man. He was a renowned figure in the king's court. He was no ordinary citizen, but he did not hide his pain at what was being plotted against God's people. He did not sit unmoved by the murderous intent of Haman; it affected him. The impact of these things filled him with deep consternation.

Then there was correspondence. When Esther was told of the actions of her cousin, she sent a messenger out from the palace with a change of clothes for him. When he refused them, the messenger was sent the second time to ascertain what was wrong. On this occasion Mordecai did two things: (i) he told the servant all that had happened and all that was being planned against the Jews, and (ii) he also gave the servant a copy of the letter that Haman had sent throughout the empire. Why did he do that? Why did he not just report the thing? Was it in case Hatach the servant would misunderstand what he said and thus misreport his words to Esther, or was it in case Esther would think it was just hearsay or rumour and dismiss it from her mind? Whatever the reason, Mordecai took the safest option and sent her a copy of the letter. He wanted her to know firsthand—with no mistakes, no misunderstanding, no misrepresentations—what was taking place. This correspondence was vitally important in dealing with the issue.

Third, there was a charge. Note the words of v. 8: "Also he gave him the copy of the writing of the decree that was given at Shushan to destroy them, to shew it unto Esther, and to declare it unto her, and to charge her that she should go in unto the king, to make supplication unto him, and to make request before him for her people."

The phrase "and to charge her" is in a form in the original Hebrew language that signifies something intentional or intense. In other words, this charge was a very serious thing. Mordecai was commanding Esther to do something urgently, deliberately, and intentionally. She was not to wait to see how things would pan out or just wait for a good opportunity to talk to the king. This threat was so serious that she needed to act with deliberate intent.

Mordecai's response to Haman's plan was both immediate and intense. He realized from the beginning that something had to be done; so he reacted as he did.

Interwoven with Mordecai's reaction was Esther's own reaction. If his was passionate, impressive, and heart stirring, Esther's became the same.

The final verses of this chapter reveal this young woman preparing to take a personal stand for God and His people with the potential of great cost to herself. Remember she was a young queen, maybe in her twenties. She was living in a godless royal family. She was surrounded by officers, leaders, and advisors who did not know God. She was part of a regime that had a terrible reputation at home and abroad. Humanly speaking there was nothing in her favour. Nevertheless, when she heard all that Mordecai had to say and understood that he was charging her to go into the king and plead for the life of her people, she indicated her willingness to go and said in the words of v. 16, "Go, gather all the Jews that are present in Shushan, and fast ye for me, and neither eat nor drink three days, night or day: I also and my maidens will fast likewise; and so will I go in unto the king: which is not according to the law: and if I perish, I perish." Powerful words: "I go...and if I perish, I perish."

These words form one of the great texts in this book. They have been used and applied in so many different settings throughout the history of the church of Christ. This phrase or something similar has been the resolve of some of God's people in times of crisis. It is a statement of purpose, a statement of decision, a statement of conviction and steadfastness and boldness, especially in the face of grave danger. And as such it is of incredible importance to every believer in Christ. These words reveal a genuine resolve to stand in an evil day, whatever personal cost may be involved. And that is what I want to examine: Faithfulness to God whatever the cost. Three headings will guide our thoughts:

FAITHFULNESS TO GOD REQUIRES SPIRITUAL COMPREHENSION.

Mordecai's reaction to Haman's plan came when (as v. 1 puts it) he "perceived all that was done." The word "perceived" means to know, or to find out and discern, or to have knowledge of. It is signifying that Mordecai understood what was happening. He could see it. He got it. There was no question in his mind. When he heard the reports and read the letter, he immediately realized that there was a very real threat facing God's covenant people.

While this was true of Mordecai from the very beginning of chapter 4, it was not true of Esther until later in the chapter. When we read vv. 1-4 carefully, we discover that though all the Jews in Persia were troubled and distraught and fearful, Esther was initially oblivious to what was taking place in the kingdom. And even when her maids and chamberlains (her servants) came and told her of Mordecai, it appears that she still had no idea what was going on. She sent Hatach out to Mordecai to find out what was happening and why he was behaving as he was. Somehow or other, Esther was not aware of Haman's plans. Whether she was sheltered from this in the palace, whether it was kept from her deliberately or whether she was preoccupied with other things is difficult to say. However, for a period of time she was ignorant of what was happening around her.

That all changed as she and Mordecai kept up their contact. The exchanges between them were instrumental in bringing her to understand what was unfolding in the empire. It is important to see this. In the course of this chapter, Esther learned that she was living in very perilous times. She learned that there was one who was set on destroying her and her people. She learned that the Persian king and government were against God's covenant nation. She learned that the very existence of the Jews was under threat. She learned that there was a very deeply rooted intolerance for Mordecai and those like him. She learned that she was surrounded by people who were plotting the death and destruction of her people.

Esther had not seen that before. But she finally understood it, and it was that comprehension that prompted her to react as she did. Like Mordecai, Esther now perceived all that was done. So, she determined to do all that she could to save her people. Her understanding of the gravity of the situation made her realize her duty in the situation.

Surely there is a lesson for us in these last days. Do we understand that, as there was an adversary in Esther's day, so we face an adversary in our day? Failure to realize that danger will translate into a failure to resist that danger. As believers we need to comprehend Satan's activity with regard to God's people:

SATAN'S PLAN FOR GOD'S PEOPLE

There is enough evidence in Scripture to underscore the point that Satan wants to destroy the church of Christ. Peter described him as being like a roaring lion, walking about seeking whom he may devour. He is a fierce opponent of all things Christian. He hates Christ, and he hates all those who belong to Christ. His plan against the church is one of destruction.

SATAN'S POWER AGAINST GOD'S PEOPLE

Haman acted against the Jews with purpose and authority from the king. He was not a weak enemy. He had power to move against them. And is that not true of Satan? He is a mighty enemy of God's people. In Ephesians 6, Paul spoke of Christians wrestling against "...principalities, against powers, against the rulers of the darkness of this world, against spiritual wickedness in high places." We have a formidable enemy who is prepared to stop at nothing in his desires against the people of God.

SATAN'S PROCEDURE WITH GOD'S PEOPLE

Haman worked by deceit and cruelty and by enlisting the help of others. Does Satan not do the same? There are many false teachers, worldlyminded people, ungodly leaders, wicked men and women who are set against the church. This will culminate in the last days in the wicked work of Antichrist towards the Lord's people.

We need to understand this. We need to be awake and alert to what is happening around us. We are in a spiritual battle that involves attack after attack upon the foundations of the gospel of Jesus Christ. People argue against the divine inspiration and thus the authority, infallibility, inerrancy and sufficiency of the Word of God. They deny the unique Person and work of the Lord Jesus Christ. Many preach against the new birth or salvation by grace alone through faith alone in Christ alone. We are in a day when the truth of Christian liberty is being turned on its head. The church is facing attack on moral issues, with some thinking that homosexuality is compatible with Christianity. There is a renewed false ecumenism, with a tendency for some to overlook the awful errors of Roman Catholicism for the sake of popularity.

What is happening? The church is under attack. We have spiritual enemies. There is a serious threat against the gospel. We need to comprehend that. We need to know the times. In 1 Chronicles 12:32, we read that "the children of Issachar...were men that had understanding of the times, to know what Israel ought to do." What is true of the church generally is true of the Christian personally. We need to appreciate that we have a great foe that will stop at nothing in his attempt to destroy us. Haman was an enemy of God's people, and Satan is an enemy to us. He would tear us from Christ if he could. He would fill our hearts with worldliness, bitterness, and spiritual coldness.

He will throw every temptation in our way and make us think we are strong enough to deal with it. He is a devious, strong, and persistent enemy of our souls. Get a hold of that! If we fail to know who our spiritual enemy is and what our spiritual enemy is doing, we will not take a stand against him. We need spiritual comprehension. God's people are being destroyed for lack of knowledge. We need to comprehend the danger.

FAITHFULNESS TO GOD REQUIRES SPIRITUAL COURAGE.

When we first meet with Esther in this book, we could never have imagined the situation that she was going to face as the queen of Persia. Things moved very quickly in her life. One moment she was just another Jewish girl, a young woman with exceptional beauty. But by the time we come into chapter 4, we discover that this young woman (probably in her late twenties) was facing the greatest crisis of her life. She and her people were under threat of death, and she was the only one who had any kind of influence over the king. However, her approach to him was not without great risk.

Persian law was strange. No one could approach the king until he asked for such a person, and he had not asked for Esther for over thirty days. Therefore, for her to go into him could mean certain execution. Esther was in a dilemma: to go to Ahasuerus might mean death, and not to go would certainly mean death. It was a life-and-death situation if ever there was one. Bravely, Esther responded, "I go...and if I perish, I perish." We need to understand the incredible courage involved in that decision.

I cannot read the words of vv. 10-14 and not pick up on the awful internal struggle that Esther must have been facing. This was not an easy decision. Generations of Jews depended on her getting this right. To do nothing was not really an option. God had brought her to the kingdom for such a time as this. Everything up until now had been for this purpose. An incredible weight of responsibility lay upon her. Her life and the lives of thousands of others rested on her decision. It took great courage for her to say, "I go...and if I perish, I perish." Esther's courage had three aspects to it:

SUBMISSION

Mordecai had charged her to do this. That is the language of v. 8. (This is not the first time we find him charging Esther and not the first time that she obeyed him—consider Esther 2:10, 20.) She had grown up obeying her cousin, and her courageous decision to go into Ahasuerus uninvited was another act of obedience. While she wrestled with the prospect of this, she was prepared to submit herself to the commands of Mordecai.

SACRIFICE

Esther was ready to put her own life on the line. This was an act of self-denial. She was willing to put herself in danger if she might spare others from danger. Clearly, she thought more of others than she did of herself.

SERVICE

Esther was the queen; she had servants to wait on her. In this case the queen became the servant and was ready to lay down her life.

I discover the same courageous spirit in the lives of the Hebrew children in Daniel 2. They would rather have been thrown into the fiery furnace than be guilty of idolatry. Daniel was just as courageous when he continued to pray even though he faced the lions' den. The apostles showed similar resolve when they said that they would obey God rather than men. In Hebrews 11, we read of men who by faith had enough courage to do right even when the world was against them.

I fear that kind of spirit is largely lacking in twenty-first-century Christianity. Could it be we have a soft view of what following Christ involves? We shy away from suffering. There is a tendency to "fit in" rather than "stand up." I have never known a time when so many firmly held Christian views are being thrown away lest offence is given. Sadly, the idea of presenting our bodies as a living sacrifice seems to be a foreign concept to many of God's people. There are few courageous enough to be different and to stand up for Jesus, few courageous enough to live a life of separation unto God and His gospel, or courageous enough to say, "I am not my own and I will go through with God whatever the cost."

This is discipleship. Christ said in Luke 14:26, 27: "If any man come to me, and hate not his father, and mother, and wife, and children, and brethren, and sisters, yea, and his own life also, he cannot be my disciple. And whosoever doth not bear his cross, and come after me, cannot be my disciple." Where has the spirit of cross-bearing gone? The enemy has come in like a flood, and we must courageously lift up Christ as the great and only Saviour of sinners.

FAITHFULNESS TO GOD REQUIRES SPIRITUAL CONFIDENCE.

I sense that Mordecai's words in v. 14 played a major part in Esther's decision to go into the king. He said to her, "If thou altogether holdest thy peace at this time, then shall there enlargement and deliverance arise to the Jews from another place; but thou and thy father's house shall be destroyed: and who knoweth whether thou art come to the kingdom for such a time as this?" What did he mean? He surely meant that God would bring deliverance to His people either through Esther or through someone else. Matthew Henry said of this text: "This was the language of a strong faith, which staggered not at the promise when the danger was most threatening, but against hope believed in hope. Instruments may fail, but God's covenant will not." Esther believed that, and in an act of faith—imperfect faith maybe but faith nonetheless—ventured forward to do what was right. That is why she called for a fast. Implicit in that was a call to prayer for divine intervention and a demonstration of confidence it would come.

We need faith in God's promise and purpose in these days. Faith is the victory that overcomes the world. Too often we walk by sight and not by faith. But we must fight the good fight of faith in faith and by faith in God who will do right.

8

Pleading at the Throne

*And it was so, when the king saw Esther the queen
standing in the court, that she obtained favour in his
sight: and the king held out to Esther the golden sceptre
that was in his hand. So Esther drew near, and touched
the top of the sceptre.*

Esther 5:2

George Lawson in his commentary on the book of Esther wisely
noted, "Esther was not one of those who resolve and promise
well, but do not perform." We know the kind of person he was
referring to: the person who pledges or commits to act in a certain
way, but then, when the time for action finally comes, fails to live
up to that promise. People like that lack faithfulness. They turn
back at the last minute and the pledge is never fulfilled.

Esther was not like that. At the end of chapter 4, this young
queen declared her readiness to go into king Ahasuerus and
plead for the Jews living in Persia.

That undertaking was fraught with huge problems. As mentioned earlier, Persian law stated that no one could come before the king unless he or she had been invited. A person daring to venture in without an invitation could be executed—and that strange law applied to the queen as well. The problem for Esther lay in the fact that—for some reason not stated in the chapter—she had not been called into the king's court for over thirty days. Therefore, for her to promise that she would go in—knowing that she could be killed—was no small undertaking. Esther did not only make that promise; she fulfilled it.

The fulfillment of that solemn pledge came after the three days of prayer and fasting that are referred to at the end of Esther 4. I say prayer and fasting, because although the word "prayer" is not used in these verses, in the Old Testament fasting rarely, if ever, stood by itself.

The word translated "fast" in Esther 4:16 first appears in Judges 20. In that chapter it is used in connection with the children of Israel seeking counsel from God, and especially asking that God would be gracious to them. They fasted as they prayed, and they prayed as they fasted. That first mention of the word sets the tone for its use throughout the Old Testament. This was a religious exercise—a time of self-denial, a deliberate season which involved setting ordinary things aside so that time and effort could be given to seeking God.

This is what Esther asked Mordecai to do and what she said she and her servants would do also. She wanted to saturate in prayer this entire effort to save the Jews.

I might just make the point that this ought to be the course of action that every child of God (and indeed the church of God) should follow in times of crisis. What should a believer do when he is faced with grave temptations? Where should he go when life is full of trials and troubles? Whom should he turn to first of all when everything around him seems to be falling apart? What should we do when everything looks hopeless and we feel helpless? We should carry our burdens to God in prayer. Set time aside, get before God, and unburden your heart to Him. Make use of your access to Him. Deny self and spend time in prayer. That has been the way of God's people throughout history, and it was the way Esther approached this crisis in her day.

Perhaps this question might arise in our minds: If God had placed her in the kingdom for such a time as this and if He was working all things together and providentially ordering all events, why did she need to pray at all? We must remember that God's providence does not remove our responsibility. If we are going to fulfill our responsibilities before God, we need His strength, His wisdom, grace, power, mercy, and His protection. Therefore we should pray. His providence and our prayers go hand in hand. Let us never fall into the snare of thinking, "Whatever will be, will be" and living as if prayer does not matter.

These three days of prayer and fasting strengthened Esther, and when this allotted time was over, she prepared herself to go in before the king and plead for her people.

That brings us into Esther 5. This chapter falls into two distinct parts. The first part (vv. 1-8) records Esther standing at the throne and interceding with the king on behalf of her people. The second part (vv. 9-14) records the sinful pride of Haman and the firming up of his plans to destroy the Jews. It is the first part that I want to examine now. This is a section that teaches us much about prayer. We will look at Esther and her predicament, and then we will consider the believer and his privilege. Remember, Esther had to go into the presence of a wicked man, but we are able to go into the presence of a God of love and mercy. She was not called, but we are invited. She went in against the law; but we can go in unto the Lord according to His promise and with His encouragement. She had no friend at court whom she could rely on; but we, even when we have sinned, have an Advocate with the Father, our Lord Jesus Christ. She had no idea whether she would be able to make her request known or not. But we have no such fear, for it is our privilege to carry everything to God in prayer. So as we look at Esther going in to the throne, we see a picture of the far greater privilege God's people have of going to His throne and seeking His blessing.

THE GRACIOUS ACCEPTANCE AT THE THRONE

When Esther stood in the inner court of the king's palace, she experienced one of the most tense moments of her entire life. Her coming into Ahasuerus uninvited could have gone either way. Remember, this was the man who divorced his first wife because she did not obey him, and there was a very real possibility that he would react against Esther because she was breaking royal protocol. When she stood there, she could not have been sure what kind of mood the king was in. Therefore, this was one of the most harrowing moments she had ever known in the palace. But on this occasion, Ahasuerus received her. Esther 5:2 outlines the steps in that reception. Consider the exact words: "And it was so, when the king saw Esther the queen standing in the court, that she obtained favour in his sight: and the king held out to Esther the golden sceptre that was in his hand. So Esther drew near, and touched the top of the sceptre." This was more than just a royal ceremony. These words speak of acceptance. They speak of approval and affection. Esther was being brought to the throne where she could speak personally with the king.

We might well ask: What was it that led the king to receive her as he did? Was it her appearance—the fact that she was dressed in royal apparel? (Obviously, she changed her clothes when coming into the king. There was nothing casual or careless about her approach into the king's presence.) Was he impressed with her beauty? Was it because she made the approach at all? Did Ahasuerus reckon that there must be something pressing on her mind to make her take such a risk? Was it because he had a desire to see her and remembered that she was his wife? The reason is not stated. Ultimately it was because the king's heart was in the hand of the Lord, and the Lord so moved that heart that Ahasuerus was kind, gracious, and receptive. God turned the king's heart, and as a result Esther was graciously accepted.

Do we not see the spiritual lesson here? This was a precarious time for Esther. Her acceptance by the king was not guaranteed. If you are a believer in Christ, you have no such uncertainty to be concerned about. There has never been a believer who has sought to draw near to God and found that the way was closed or that God refused him. We have access to the throne of God. As believers in Christ we are accepted by the King of glory. Having come to Christ by faith, we will never be cast out. The child of God has a glorious acceptance by the Father. Let me expand on that truth:

OUR ACCEPTANCE WITH GOD IS GUARANTEED BECAUSE OF CHRIST'S RIGHTEOUSNESS.

According to v. 1, Esther was accepted by the king as she was wearing her royal apparel. Those were the garments the king provided for her—her royal robes. She was dressed in a particular way that was acceptable to the king. Does that not remind us of the truth of our justification? Justification is an act of God's grace whereby He pardons or forgives all our sins and accepts us as righteous in His sight. But why?

It is because of the righteousness of Christ that is imputed to us and that we receive by faith alone. In other words, when we approach God, we do so clothed in the righteousness of Jesus Christ, and because of Him we are accepted. God no longer looks upon us in our sin or our self-righteousness. He no longer looks upon us in our guilt or our defilement. He looks upon us in Christ. Our union with Christ means we are brought in. We are no longer strangers. We have been declared righteous in Christ; therefore, we are as accepted by the Father as Christ Himself is. It is a staggering truth. Christ's righteousness is counted as ours. The hymn writer put it well with the words, "Jesus, thy blood and righteousness my beauty are, my glorious dress...." This has been reckoned to our account. Therefore, as Paul notes in Ephesians 1:6, we are accepted in the beloved; that is, we are accepted in Christ. His imputed righteousness guarantees our reception.

OUR ACCEPTANCE WITH GOD RESULTS IN THE RIGHT TO DRAW NEAR:

Esther's procession is outlined here. In v. 1 she stood in the inner court. In v. 2 she drew near. In v. 3 she is standing by the king talking with him. Her acceptance brought her nigh. The phrase "draw near" is very significant. It means "to approach, to be at hand, or to join." It is a word that suggests closeness.

It is first used in the Old Testament in relation to Abraham and is found in Genesis 18. When the Lord visited Abraham and relayed to him that He was going to destroy Sodom and Gomorrah because of their wickedness, we are told in v. 23 that Abraham drew near and said, "Wilt thou also destroy the righteous with the wicked?" His drawing near to the Lord was in connection with prayer, and this is the great privilege of the Christian. The Psalmist said in Psalm 73:28, "But it is good for me to draw near to God." God does not keep the Christian at arm's length; He draws us close. We can come right into the presence of the King Himself. We can stand before Him. In Christ we have a Mediator, and through Him we have this glorious opportunity.

OUR ACCEPTANCE WITH GOD IS SUCH THAT IT ALLAYS OUR FEARS.

As soon as the king held out his golden scepter, any fear Esther had of being refused or repelled or, worse, executed was gone. She was accepted; therefore she had no need to fear. This is true for the believer in Christ: "For as many as are led by the Spirit of God, they are the sons of God. For ye have not received the spirit of bondage again to fear; but ye have received the Spirit of adoption, whereby we cry, Abba, Father" (Romans 8:14-16). Satan would make us stay away from the throne of grace and fill us with fear. But we have no need to fear as we approach heaven's court.

When I read that Esther obtained favour, I cannot help but think of the favour and grace Christians enjoy in Jesus Christ. You will note that she came on the third day. The third day often points to resurrection day. It was on the third day of creation that dry land appeared and the earth brought forth the grass and trees and plants; there was life. And it was on the third day that Christ rose from the dead. As believers, we have acceptance with God because we stand on resurrection ground. Christ has lived for us, died for us, risen for us, entered into heaven with His own blood for us, is seated at His Father's right hand for us, and pleads for us. Because of Him, we have acceptance.

Hebrews 9:12 tells that after Christ had obtained eternal redemption for His people, He entered into the holiest place with

His own blood. In Hebrews 10:19, we are reminded that we have boldness to enter into the holiest by the blood of Jesus. Verse 22 follows that up with the words, "Let us draw near with a true heart...." We have a gracious acceptance at the throne of God because of Christ.

THE GREAT ASSURANCE AT THE THRONE

The turning point in these verses came when Esther drew near and touched the top of the sceptre. That was hugely significant. It was a sign that she was welcome. It marked her right to stand before the king and make her requests and petitions known to him. However, that was not the only encouragement of assurance that Esther received. The king also spoke words of assurance. "Then said the king unto her, "What wilt thou, Queen Esther? And what is thy request? It shall be given thee to the half of the kingdom." (v. 3) Those are interesting words. Note the threefold assurance of these verses:

THE KING WAS READY TO HEAR HER REQUEST.

He asked her, "What wilt thou and what is thy request?" In other words, he was inviting her to make her requests known to him. There was no harshness here—no bitterness—nothing but a genuine desire to have her unburden her heart to him. And is that not true of Christ? There are repeated references in Scripture where He invites us and encourages us to make our requests known unto Him.

Take as one example Philippians 4:6, "Be careful for nothing; but in every thing by prayer and supplication with thanksgiving let your requests be made known unto God." Believer, our God and Saviour invites us to call upon him in our days of trouble. He invites us to open our mouths wide and He will fill them. He invites us to draw near to His throne and pray without ceasing. He invites us to come with boldness, liberty, and freedom of speech to the throne of grace. This is His great encouragement to us. In the Song of Solomon the word is, "Let me hear thy voice." That is what our great King says to us.

THE KING HAD THE MEANS TO ENRICH HER ABUNDANTLY.

Consider v. 3 and v. 6 carefully. He was promising her up to half of his kingdom. Those words should be read in connection with the words of Esther 1:4 "...he shewed the riches of his glorious kingdom and the honour of his excellent majesty many days." It took Ahasuerus many days to show off the riches of his kingdom. Remember, his empire stretched over 127 provinces. He was a very wealthy man—the wealthiest in the world at that time. Therefore, he had the ability and the abundance to enrich Esther. And he made that known to her. Nevertheless, what he had and what he said are nothing in comparison to the riches that are available to us in Christ. Ephesians 1 speaks of the riches of His glory or the riches of His grace. His resources can never be exhausted. John Newton picked up on this when he said,

> *Come, my soul, thy suit prepare,*
> *Jesus loves to answer prayer;*
> *He Himself has bid thee pray,*
> *Therefore will not say thee nay.*
> *Thou art coming to a King,*
> *Large petitions with thee bring;*
> *For His grace and pow'r are such,*
> *None can ever ask too much.*

THE KING ANSWERED HER PETITIONS.

Notice what Esther asked for in verse 4. "If it seem good unto the king, let the king and Haman come this day unto the banquet that I have prepared for him." Ahasuerus granted her petition. Her entire request was granted, not just once but twice. What an encouragement this must have been to her. She was now assured that she had the ear of the king and that he would be responsive to her pleas.

Take that to an even higher level, for is this not true of the Lord also? He gives us assurances and encouragements and helps as we pray. He invites us to His throne of grace and meets us at the point of our need. We have every reason to come to Him. If Ahasuerus—a wicked man—assured Esther, how much more does our God and King not assure us? Believer pray—and pray again.

THE GODLY ATTITUDE BEFORE THE THRONE

Everything about Esther in these verse shows a respectful, humble, and meek spirit. She did not rush into the king's presence but waited on him. Her words were also carefully prepared. Esther came to the king with a well-thought-out request and presented it in a clear and expectant manner.

There are lessons for all Christians with regard to their attitude towards prayer. Prayer is a gracious privilege and one which we should approach with careful preparation. Humility, patience, meekness, and trust are never out of place as we draw near to God. While it is true that we can pray in any circumstance and sometimes in the midst of a conversation, as in the case of Nehemiah, it is important for God's people that we prepare our hearts and our words. We ought to pray for grace to pray better.

As I draw this chapter to a close, there is one further observation to be made: While the Jews in Persia were facing death, they had someone in the king's court pleading for them. Haman was working against them, but Esther was working for them. In an infinitely greater sense, the Christian has something far better. We face an implacable enemy. Satan, the accuser of the brethren, seeks to devour and destroy us, and, truth be told, we are no match for him. However, we have One who pleads for us before His Father's throne. Christ ever lives to make intercession for His people. As our High Priest, He pleads the merit of His work on our behalf. Christ's prayers are always answered. He is our Advocate, Mediator, Redeemer, and Saviour: therefore, all is well.

For Such a Time as This

9

The Sinner's Four Great Problems

Then went Haman forth that day joyful and with a glad heart: but when Haman saw Mordecai in the king's gate, that he stood not up, nor moved for him, he was full of indignation against Mordecai.

Esther 5:9

Esther 5 outlines, in some considerable detail, the great contrast between Queen Esther and Haman, the prime-minister of Persia. Although these two people had a number of things in common, they were very different people. For example, both were very close to the king; both were active in the royal palace; both occupied powerful positions in the Persian Empire. And, therefore, both had tremendous influence in the kingdom. However, in Esther 5, the contrast between them comes to the surface.

On one hand, we have the account of Esther going in before the king to plead for her people. And in these verses, we discover her to be a person of incredible faith, courage, and boldness.

Although she was a young woman facing a dangerous situation, Esther showed a level of maturity that is both impressive and instructive.

Esther did not venture forward in her own strength. She had enough sense to know that she could only take this stand with the help of God, so she bathed the whole endeavour in prayer. When Esther took these bold steps and stood in the king's court, she was acting by faith. There she was—isolated and in danger—but she was obedient, steadfast, meek, humble, and committed.

She was an example of a faithful servant. And as such she conveys a message to the young believers reading this. There is a work that God has for you to do. He has providentially brought you into the world at this time. This is your day for service. He has given you certain gifts, and your chief end in life is to glorify Him and enjoy Him for ever.

When Paul wrote to Timothy, he told him, "Let no man despise thy youth; but be thou an example of the believers, in word, in conversation, in charity, in spirit, in faith, in purity" (1 Timothy 4:12). The word "despise" means to think against. It comes from two words that mean think and down. It is as if Paul is saying to Timothy, "Do not let your youthfulness hinder your service for God. Do not let others despise you for that."

What he was stressing is that God often uses young people to do a great work for him. Remember, Samuel was a young boy when God called him to serve Him. Gideon was the youngest and least in his family when God used him to deliver His people. David was a young man when he was anointed king. Solomon was not very old when he was placed on the throne. Throughout church history God has been pleased to save young people, fill them with His Spirit, and use them in His work. Some of the world's greatest preachers started to preach when they were teenagers. It is possible for a young Christian to be marked with virtue, honour, faithfulness, obedience, courage, and to live with a true and godly fear of the Lord. Who knows whether God has brought you to the kingdom for such a time as this?

So, on one hand, we discover Esther—a woman of faith, courage and boldness—but on the other hand, we discover Haman. He was the exact opposite. When we first meet with him in Esther 3, he appears as a proud, petulant, and pompous person.

He had a bad temper, a very inflated view of himself, and a cruel streak running through him. He was an arrogant man, full of anger and bitterness towards the Jews living in Persia, and he had a heart and mind ready to hatch a plan of genocide against those Jews. There is nothing nice or pleasant or good about him.

Those character traits that are so evident in Esther 3 are brought to the surface again in Esther 5. If Esther was a godly woman, Haman was an ungodly man. If Esther was meek, patient, and selfless, he was brash, impudent, and extremely selfish. If Esther waited on God, Haman was ready to do war with God. He was a sinful man, and it is as if the Holy Spirit has sharpened His pencil and drawn in the details of his life for us to see.

Thomas McCrie, in his commentary of the book of Esther, noted, "It is not pleasant to go home with Haman; but God thinks it good for us to see the inside of a bad man's heart." I might add that we not only see inside a bad man's heart—we see the outside of a bad man's life and the foolish advice of a bad man's world. And it is not a pretty picture.

However, we cannot ignore it. According, to 1 Corinthians 10:11, these things have been written for our admonition. They have been recorded for our learning that we might be warned and taught, not just by exhortation but by example. When I look at Haman in Esther 5, I see a picture of a sinner who is pursuing a life of sin and who is on course to suffer a terrible death. These are important verses for they reveal to us the sinner's four great problems.

THE SELFISH IDOLATRY THAT PLAGUES THE SINNER

Even the most casual reading of these verses turns up the truth that Haman was a self-centered, proud and egotistic man. We get a hint of that back in Esther 3, when he flew into a rage when Mordecai would not bow down to him or reverence him. The depth of his pride is more clearly seen in Esther 5.

In v. 5, he is called to the first banquet that Esther asked for. Then in v. 8, he is invited to another banquet the next day. It was that private invitation that gives context to the words of v. 9:

"Then went Haman forth that day joyful and with a glad heart." The fact he had been invited to a banquet with the king and queen filled him with excitement.

I picture him leaving the palace courtyard with a spring in his step, a proud, gloating, happy look on his face, his chest sticking out, and his mind racing with high thoughts of himself. When he got home (after being angry with Mordecai on the way) he sent for his wife and called for his friends to come so that he could tell them all that had happened. (The words "sent" and "called" in v. 10 are important. They mean that he directed them to come and had them brought.) He could not wait to tell them what was going on. When they came, he told them of all the glory of his riches, the number of children he had, and all the favours he had received of the king and how he had been advanced in the royal court. Then in v. 12, he topped it all off by saying, "and moreover, yea, Esther the queen did let no man come in with the king unto the banquet that she had prepared but myself; and tomorrow am I invited unto her also with the king."

Once he got his audience, he began to boast and brag about himself. It was all about him—his fortune; his family; his fame; his friendships; his future. (The very reference to his many children seems needless. Did his wife and friends not know how many children he had? But in Persian culture the more children you had, the wealthier you were considered to be.) The man could not stop talking about himself. He was a proud man, and he wanted everyone to know how great he thought he was. There is not a reference about God or others who have helped him. There is nothing about his family's support. It is all about Haman. Haman's life revolved around Haman.

He worshipped himself. What is self-worship but idolatry? The first commandment addresses this very matter when it states, "Thou shalt have no other gods before me." (Exodus 20:3) What is forbidden in that commandment? The Westminster Shorter Catechism answers that question with these words: "The first commandment forbiddeth the denying, or not worshiping and glorifying, the true God as God, and our God; and the giving of that worship and glory to any other, which is due to Him alone."

That is exactly what Haman did. He did not worship God; he worshipped himself. His proud heart was full of self. Pride and idolatry go hand in hand. It has been well said that "pride was the first sin that entered into the universe. It was pride that turned angels into devils. It was pride that, after thinning heaven and peopling hell, invaded our world, and drove man out of paradise. Pride has marred the work of God, given birth to infidelity, apostasy, impiety, blasphemy, and persecution. It is the mother of heresy." Pride gives birth to idolatry.

This plague is in the heart of every person. Remember what Christ said in John 4:23: "But the hour cometh, and now is, when the true worshippers shall worship the Father in spirit and in truth: for the Father seeketh such to worship him." What does that infer? By nature, men and women do not worship God. The Father seeks and saves sinners in order for that to happen; but by nature, man is a self-worshipper. He is proud and full of himself. God is not in all his thoughts. Sinful man loves himself more than he loves God. That is why he rejects the gospel. That is why he loves the world and the things of the world—because they feed self. The human heart is full of self-centeredness, and every sinner will die an unsaved selfish sinner, unless saved by God's grace.

THE SINFUL INDIGNATION THAT MARS THE SINNER

From a human perspective, Haman had everything. He was the prime minister of the greatest empire in the world. He had riches far beyond what others could ever have hoped for. He had a wife and many children. He enjoyed prestige, power, and position. He had the ear of the king and had access to the royal throne. Others looking on would think, "He has nothing to complain about!" However, notice v. 9, and observe how quickly this man's mood changes: "Then went Haman forth that day joyful and with a glad heart: but when Haman saw Mordecai in the king's gate, that he stood not up, nor moved for him, he was full of indignation against Mordecai." He went from being joyful to being incensed in just a few steps.

It is worth noting Mordecai's actions here. In Esther 3, he refused to bow before Haman. As we considered earlier, Mordecai would not give him worship that was due to the Lord alone, and the fact that Haman was an Agagite added to his refusal to honour him—and so it was at that time that Haman moved the king to pass a law to kill all the Jews. Mordecai knew that law had been passed, but even then he was still refusing to bow before Haman. The threat of death did not stop him from being faithful to God.

When Mordecai refused to bow, Haman was incensed. The phrase, "he was full of indignation" means that he was angry—full of anger—so he went into a rage. Note how quickly that happened. One minute he was happy and full of joy; the next he was angry and full of indignation. Needless to say, nothing had really changed in his life. He was still the prime minister. He was still close to the king. He still had an invitation from the queen. He was still rich and powerful, and Mordecai was the same Mordecai. But Haman was enraged. What happened? He did not have everything he wanted. His ego was stroked one minute and he was glad; but when it was insulted the next, he was angry. The root cause of his anger was the sinfulness of his heart.

It has been said, "To make a man happy whose heart is astray from God is impossible." George Lawson in his commentary on Esther said,

> Give a whole world of pleasure to a man who loves the world and the things of it, he will soon find that something is wanted, though perhaps he does not know, so well as Haman thought he did, what it is. He finds some gall and wormwood that spread poison over his pleasures. All his abundance cannot compensate for the loss of some one thing or other that he deems essential to his happiness. The fact is that the world cannot give a right constitution to his disordered soul, or be a substitute for that Divine favour in which lies the life of our souls.[5]

To put it simply, there lies at the heart of the sinner a deep sense of unhappiness. Sometimes it is covered up but it is there.

5   George Lawson, *Discourses on the Whole Book of Esther: To which are Added, Sermons*, on ... 42. See https://books.google.com/books?id=SC4fAAAAYAAJ

He is angry with God, at times he is angry with others, and he is often angry with himself.

Though the sinner may have much of what this world can give him, there is still something wrong with him. He is never really satisfied. Do we not see that in the life of the prodigal son spoken of in Luke 15? He had a loving father, a comfortable home, a meaningful role in the family, riches and wealth at his disposal, but he left it all for the far country. For a time he thought he was happy, but when the famine came he "began to be in want."

The sinner is in want. He wants peace. He wants freedom from guilt. He wants purpose and meaning. He wants joy in his soul. However, the world cannot give him that; therefore, he is filled with anger. I know young people and older people, and this is how it is with them. They are angry. They feel God owes them something. The problem lies within their own hearts—and it is sin. Haman was an indignant man; it was just another part of his iniquity.

THE SPIRITUAL IGNORANCE THAT BLINDS THE SINNER

When I read this section of the chapter, one of the first thoughts that struck me was the fact that while Haman was filled with joy and his heart was glad, things were actually moving against him. Remember the context of these words. The king had signed Haman's desire to kill all the Jews into law, and that had caused consternation among Mordecai and the other Jews in the empire. Mordecai, in turn, sent word to Esther, urging her to go into the king and plead for her people. The king accepted her and responded positively to her request to call a banquet. It is obvious what Esther was planning on doing. She was going to expose Haman's plans before the king and make it clear that if his wishes were carried out, she would be put to death. We can tell what the king's reaction would be. We find it in Esther 6. The very next day, when the king heard these details, he ordered the death of Haman.

The timing of this is almost incredible. This was Haman's last full day on earth. He was happy and full of himself. In fact, I think he was pretty pleased with himself and most likely he believed he was invincible. What could stop him now? What could hinder his plan being carried out? What could happen that would mean any change in direction? Little did he know the king was about to move against him in deadly judgment. He was ignorant of all that God was doing behind the scenes.

Is that not a problem with sinners? They boast of tomorrow. They think all is well with them. They lay plans for months and years to come. They go about their lives with a smug sense of, "I'm doing okay. There is nothing for me to worry about," while at the same time they are blind to the fact that there is but a step between them and death, and that they are under the wrath of the great God and king of Heaven. The sinner is ignorant of his danger, ignorant of how close he is to a lost hell, ignorant of the fact that God's arrows of judgment are trained upon him. The god of this world has blinded the minds of unbelievers so that they do not believe the gospel. They are happy, but they do not seem to know that they are on the way to death. What is that but false security? The sinner rejoices in the things of this world, without due consideration being given to the things of the next world. Is that where you are today?

THE SENSELESS INSTRUCTION THAT MISDIRECTS THE SINNER

As we close this section, notice the advice Haman received from his wife and friends. "Then said Zeresh his wife and all his friends unto him, Let a gallows be made of fifty cubits high, and to morrow speak thou unto the king that Mordecai may be hanged thereon: then go thou in merrily with the king unto the banquet" (Esther 5:14). Those closest to Haman gave him three pieces of advice. One, order the building of a gallows; two, speak to the king and request the execution of Mordecai; and three, go happily to the banquet. None of this was good advice. Faithful friends would have told him otherwise. Haman's problem was not Mordecai—it was Haman; yet no one had the courage to confront him with that. He was given instruction that horribly confirmed him in his perverse and sinful course. Haman was terribly lacking an honest counsellor. He was encouraged in his sin instead of being exhorted to flee from his sin. And, of course, he was thankful for the direction they gave him.

Sadly, we live in times when many are misdirected with regard to the great need of their souls. I write these words just after attending a funeral service where there was no gospel message given to the congregation. The speaker did not address the subject of the people's sin or their need of a Saviour. It was a wasted opportunity. It is imperative upon ministers of the gospel to speak the truth in love. Calling for repentance and faith in Christ are essential parts of gospel preaching. Anything else is misinformation and does a great disservice to God and to those who hear. Haman was not surrounded by faithful friends. It is my prayer that the church would ever proclaim the necessity of repentance and saving faith in Christ.

10

The Perfect

Providence of God

*On that night could not the king sleep, and he
commanded to bring the book of records of the
chronicles; and they were read before the king.*

Esther 6:1

In Proverbs 27:1, King Solomon stated, "Boast not thyself of to-morrow; for thou knowest not what a day many bring forth." His choice of words in that statement is very important. The word "boast" means to glory in. When it is connected with the word "thyself" as in "boast not thyself" it is very personal. It is a warning that individuals should never take it upon themselves to glory in something. In this case they are being warned not to glory themselves in another day or boast themselves of tomorrow. It is a very solemn warning, and the reason for such a statement is simple: We do not know what a day will bring forth. We are not to boast of the future—not even the near future—because we have no idea if we will have a tomorrow and if we do, we have no idea what that day will hold for us. We must not presume on certain things. Sometimes our tomorrows never come—and at other times we face things we never expected. We must not boast of that which is not ours.

That truth is well illustrated between the closing verse of Esther 5 and the opening verse of Esther 6. At the end of Esther 5 we discover Haman, the bloodthirsty enemy of God's people, in a very jubilant mood. Earlier that day, he had been invited to a private banquet with King Ahasuerus and Queen Esther. Esther 5:6 describes it as a "banquet of wine," and in true Persian fashion it would have been a lavish affair with an abundance of meat and fruit and wine. During that feast, Ahasuerus asked Esther what was on her mind. Why had she called for the banquet? What was her request or what did she want him to do for her? For some reason, not stated in chapter 5, Esther simply asked the king to come with Haman to another banquet the following day.

That second invitation to dine with the king and his queen filled Haman with pride and temporary happiness. He took that to be a good omen. He interpreted this private audience with the royal couple to be a sign that he was a special person. I think that feeling of "specialness" accounts for the words of Esther 5:9 where we are told that Haman "went forth that day, joyful and with a glad heart."

The events of that day pleased this proud man. He was full of himself and full of high expectations concerning the next day's events. He was on an emotional high as he left the palace. Haman was momentarily happy—and I say *momentarily* happy because no sooner had he left the royal court than he came across Mordecai the Jew. And when Mordecai refused to stand up for him or show any reverence to him, Haman became angry. However, this time, instead of flying into a rage, he refrained himself and made his way home.

He was still incensed. At that moment, Haman was obsessed with the actions of Mordecai. Although he already had the king's permission to put all the Jews to death on the twelfth month of the year, Haman longed to put Mordecai to death as soon as possible.

And that is where evil minds met. For at the end of Esther 5, Haman's wife and all of his friends told him to have fifty-cubit-high gallows made and then speak to the king in the morning to get his permission to hang Mordecai on those gallows without further delay. The chapter closes with the comment that the thing pleased Haman, and he caused the gallows to be made. Those words describe a man who was fully convinced that the next day was going to be a day of reckoning for Mordecai. He was confident that, within a few hours, his troubles with this obstinate Jew would be a thing of the past. This was a night of high expectation for Haman.

It was a proud boast, and a boast he should never have made. What was it Solomon said? "Boast not thyself of tomorrow; for thou knowest not what a day may bring forth." And so it proved. For while Esther 5 finishes with men spending the night building gallows at Haman's request, Esther 6 opens by telling us that on the very same night the king could not sleep. And from that sleepless night a series of events unfolded that eventually led to Haman being hanged on his own gallows. He thought he knew what that day would bring, but he was completely wrong. Charles Bridges once noted, "Haman plumed himself upon the prospect of the queen's banquet but was hanged like a dog before the night."

Central to the overthrow of Haman and his plans was the fact that God—and not Haman—was in control of all things. That is the outstanding lesson of Esther 6. This is a chapter of irony. It is a chapter of one man's deliverance followed by another man's demise. It is a chapter of ongoing divine intervention in the affairs of men—a chapter of irresistible power—a chapter which underscores the great contrast between the Mighty God of Heaven and a puny man of earth. These verses clearly and consistently show us the perfect providence of God. There is a wealth of encouragement and comfort for God's people here, so let us examine the details of the chapter with that thought before us—the perfect providence of God.

God's Providence Extends to Every Detail of Life.

Perhaps it is good for us at the very beginning to define what is meant by the word providence. This is not the same as good fortune, or chance, or fate, or good luck. The world thinks that things just happen—that the events of life are all haphazard and everything takes place by coincidence. But divine providence is nothing like that. The word providence comes from a Latin word meaning foresight or forethought, and it signifies the efficient administration by the all-wise God of His eternal decree. It is a word that speaks of God directing all things to their appointed end. It highlights His authority and sovereignty and the fact that He ordains whatsoever comes to pass. That aspect of God's ongoing work is visibly seen in Esther 6. There are seven things in this chapter that indicate the extent of God's providence:

THE SLEEPLESSNESS OF THE KING

We are not told that this was a common problem for the king. In fact, we are not told anything about his sleep patterns except that on this particular night—the night when Haman's gallows were being made and the night before Haman was going to come and ask to be allowed to kill Mordecai—the king could not sleep. The marginal reading puts it that "the king's sleep fled away." The thought is that there was nothing he could do to keep it. It was impossible for the king to sleep that night. Whatever he tried to do, all the usual cures for insomnia had no impact on him; he could not sleep. We know from Psalm 127:2 that the Lord gives His beloved sleep. He can also withhold sleep, and in this case Ahasuerus who was the king of a vast empire and who could order and command a thousand men to do a thousand things had no power over his own body. This was providential.

IN HIS SLEEPLESSNESS HE REQUESTED GOVERNMENT RECORDS TO BE READ.

Why did he not ask for musicians to come? Why did he not ask for some food or drink? Why did he not engage in some light reading? Why turn to the records of the empire? Did he think that would put him to sleep? If he did, even that did not work.

For the sense of the words in v. 1, where it states that "they were read before the king" means that they read them all night—right to the morning. The request for and the reading of the book of records was all of God.

When v. 2 records that "it was found written that Mordecai had told of Bigthana and Teresh," (men who were plotting to kill the king, Esther 2:21-23), we are not to think that the man reading the book went looking for this detail. He did not search for Mordecai's name. Rather, in the course of his reading, he came to that particular part of the book. The word "found" actually means to come forth to or to appear. The thought is that this record was here, and the reader came to it. He could have stopped reading before this record or he could have started to read after that part and missed this. But he was directed by the providence of God to come to that particular place in the book.

THE KING DISCOVERED THAT NIGHT THAT MORDECAI HAD NEVER BEEN REWARDED.

It was customary in Persia for the king to honour those who had been favourable to him, but no such reward or recognition had been given to Mordecai at the time. That was strange. For the king knew of his good work back then. However, all those months had passed, and this had never been addressed by the king until now. The king realised the error of that. So that meant that, right then, in the very night when Haman was planning to kill him, Mordecai and the need to honour him was foremost in the king's mind. How can we account for that without speaking of the providence of God?

THE SUDDEN APPEARANCE OF HAMAN AT THAT EARLY HOUR OF THE MORNING

Read vv. 3, 4, and 5 together. "And the king said, What honour and dignity hath been done to Mordecai for this? Then said the king's servants that ministered unto him, There is nothing done for him." (v. 4) "And the king said, Who is in the court? Now Haman was come into the outward court of the king's house, to speak unto the king to hang Mordecai on the gallows that he had prepared for him. And the king's servants said unto him, Behold, Haman standeth in the court." Note the links. "There is nothing done for him...and the king said who is in the court?" Haman appeared at that very moment. Haman had not been invited. He hadn't been sent for. But he came—and he had come to speak about killing Mordecai. That was providential—then note:

THE KING DID NOT MENTION THE MAN'S NAME HE WISHED TO HONOUR.

In v. 6 he asked, "What shall be done to the man...?" Why did he not say Mordecai's name? There was no real reason for Ahasuerus not to name him—but he was providentially restrained.

THE ANSWER GIVEN BY HAMAN WOULD LEAD TO THE HONOUR OF MORDECAI

Haman was under the impression the king was thinking of him (vv. 6-10). How wrong he was.

It is impossible to explain these things apart from the sovereignty and providence of God. Every minute detail was under God's control. If one of these things had been different—if the king had slept through the night or if the reader had read a different part of the book, or if Haman had come earlier, or if the king had said he was going to honour Mordecai—the whole outcome would have been different. But God was ordering all things. He was controlling the sleep patterns of the king, the reading habits of the officer, and the actions of Haman. Everything was under His superintendence. What does that teach us? It surely teaches us that God's providence extends to every aspect of our lives. The Westminster Confession of Faith carries this statement: "God, the great creator of all things, doth uphold, direct, dispose and govern all creatures, actions and things from the greatest even to the least, by His most wise and holy providence."[6] There is not one department of life that is outside the hand of God. He is not sovereign over some; He is sovereign over all. He does not just

---

6   The Westminster Confession of Faith, Chapter 5.1

oversee and overrule in the lives of *His* people; He overrules the lives of *all* people.

Our times are in His hands. He can turn our thoughts. He can order things that we have not considered. And the interesting thing in this chapter is that it is done quietly and almost behind the scenes. There are times when God intervenes dramatically in the lives of His people. He opened the Red Sea for Moses and the Israelites. That was a miraculous, powerful, and dramatic intervention. However, there are other times (and this is the case most of the time) when He simply works quietly and almost unnoticed. He uses ordinary means to accomplish His extraordinary purposes, but He is still working all things together for good. These men did not consider that God was at work, but they were fulfilling God's will. Is that not what Solomon meant when he said, in Proverbs 21:1 "The king's heart is in the hand of the Lord, as the rivers of water: he turneth it whithersoever he will." God's providence is over all things. If you are a believer, see that God is in control of every detail of your life! If you are an unbeliever, see that God is in control! God's providence extends to every detail of life.

God Exercises His Providence for the Good of His People.

Why did God move in these mysterious ways? Or, to put that question another way, why does God order events like these? Why does He intervene in the affairs of people? Why does He do what He does? Ultimately, He does it for His own glory. God's works glorify Him, and that includes His works of providence. He does what He does for His own honour, but also for the good of His people. The Puritan John Flavel said in his famous work, *The Mystery of Providence*, "All the results and issues of providence are profitable and beneficial to the saints."[7] In other words, God works in mysterious ways as He takes care of and blesses His own people. Everything He does is for our benefit.

In the chapter on Providence the Westminister Confession of Faith states, "As the providence of God doth in general, reach to all creatures; so, after a most special manner, it taketh care of

7 *The Works of John Flavel,* Vol. 4, Edinburgh, Banner of Truth, 345

his church and disposeth all things to the good thereof."[8] God's perfect providence takes care of the church and is for its good. That is in full agreement with the teaching of Scripture: "And we know that all things work together for good to them that love God, to them who are the called according to his purpose" (Romans 8:28). This is what David said in Psalm 57:2: "I will cry unto God most high; unto God that performeth [or completes] all things for me." He works for the good of His people. That was certainly the case in the book of Esther. God was orchestrating everything for the benefit of Esther and Mordecai and the Jews. He had their interests at heart. Everything was working together for their good! Think of that in terms of the following:

GOD'S GRACE

Remember God was working for the good of His people, even though they were not where they should have been. Other Jews had returned to Jerusalem, whereas these Jews had remained in Persia and had to one degree or another become accustomed to life there. They were part of Persian society. They were God's covenant people but had not lived like God's covenant people. Even though that was the case, God was graciously and tenderly working all things together for their benefit. God does not forsake or forget His people even when they sin against Him.

GOD'S FAITHFULNESS

When God first chose the Jews for Himself, He covenanted to bless them and to make them a blessing. When speaking to Abraham, He said that He would curse those who cursed them and bless those who blessed them. These events in Esther 6 indicate the fulfillment of that word. God keeps His promises to His people. His providence and His promises go hand in hand. It is interesting to note that when Psalm 57:2 states "I will cry unto God most high; unto God that performeth [or completes] all things for me," it has the sense that He performs all things that He has promised for me. He is a covenant keeping God.

---

8 The Westminster Confession of Faith, 5:7

Everything God does is stamped with divine wisdom. He is the all-wise Governor of all the affairs of this world. God never acts foolishly, thoughtlessly or irrationally.

This is something we need to recognize in our own lives. God moves in mysterious ways His wonders to perform; but He performs those wonders for His glory and our good. Whatever God ordains will be for the good of His people. Christ is not only Head of His church; He is Head over all things to His church. We are under His constant care. That is what is happening in Esther 6. All that was taking place was being done to bless His own covenant people. Providence is for us.

NOTHING CAN FRUSTRATE OR FOIL GOD'S PROVIDENTIAL WORK.

Haman could not frustrate or foil what was unfolding. He was absolutely powerless. These things were in God's control and not in his. He thought he was in charge, but he was dreadfully mistaken. Even his wife and family began to realise that.

Haman was a powerful man in the court of Persia, but he was not a powerful man in the court of heaven. In many ways, he reminds me of the Egyptian Pharaoh who refused to let God's people go from bondage. Pharaoh exercised great power over them, but God exercised a greater power over him. The point that is underscored in Esther 6 is that nothing and no one can stop God accomplishing His own purposes. There is nothing too hard for Him. He is God alone and since there is none beside Him or above Him, or beyond Him, His purposes will ripen and His will shall be done. This truth provides sound encouragement for God's people. It reminds us that we can trust God to do all things well. As the hymn writer so well stated:

> *Day by day and with each passing moment,*
> *Strength I find to meet my trials here;*
> *Trusting in my Father's wise bestowment,*
> *I've no cause for worry or for fear.*
> *He whose heart is kind beyond all measure*
> *Gives unto each day what He deems best,*

> *Lovingly its part of pain and pleasure,*
> *Mingling toil with peace and rest.*[9]

Furthermore, the unfrustratable providence of God confirms that Christ will be glorifed and His enemies will be defeated. This is God's eternal purpose. According to Genesis 3:15, the seed of the woman, (a reference to Christ) would bruise the serpent's head (a reference to the fact that Satan would be defeated by Christ). It may seem, at times, in this evil world, that Satan has the upper hand. However, we must not lose sight of the fact that God is working all things together for the eternal fulfilment of His plans. Satan is a defeated foe and Christ will continue to build His church.

This leads me to note one final thing in this chapter: The victorious providence of God is another reason to praise Him and rejoice in all His ways. Is it not heartening to read Esther 6 and observe the mysterious but marvellous works of God? Our response? "Bless the LORD O my soul, and all that is within me, bless his holy name."

---

9   Lina Sandell, *Day by Day*, Translated by A. L. Skoog

11

The Fall of a Foolish Sinner

*So Haman came in. And the king said unto him, What
shall be done unto the man whom the king delighteth
to honour? Now Haman thought in his heart, To whom
would the king delight to do honour
more than to myself?*

Esther 6:6

In John Bunyan's *The Pilgrim's Progress*, there is a captivating
episode involving Christian and Faithful in Vanity Fair. These
two pilgrims had just emerged from the wilderness when they
learned that they had to travel through this particular place on
their way to the Celestial city. Vanity Fair was an ancient town
where all kinds of things were bought and sold. As its name suggests it was a vain place—a place full of cheats, liars, entertain-
ers, criminals, and villains. Bunyan says that, "at this Fair are all
kinds of merchandise sold, things such as houses, lands, trades,
places, honors, preferments, titles, countries, kingdoms, lusts,

pleasures, and delights of all sorts, as harlots, wives, husbands, children, masters, servants, lives, blood, bodies, souls, silver, gold, pearls, precious stones, and what not."

Then he added that at all times you could see, "fools and rogues" and as well as "thefts, murders, adulteries, false-swearers, and that of a blood-red colour." Vanity Fair was a wicked town—a godless place. It was just like the world of today where every kind of sinful, wicked, evil thing is on offer, and there is no shortage of people ready to love pleasure more than God.

As this town lay on the way to the celestial city, Christian and Faithful had no option but go through it. Their experience there was anything but pleasant. In fact, they were arrested and charged with causing a disturbance, and, as a result of their arrest, they were beaten, covered in dirt, and thrown into a cage. They became a spectacle in the centre of the town. The townspeople gathered to gape at them, laugh at them, and accuse them of all kinds of things. At last they were brought before a court of sorts and charged with causing an uproar in the town. They were beaten again, chained, and then dragged up and down the streets so that people could attack them. Then they were brought back to their cage.

Sometime later, they were brought before the Judge—a man by the name of Lord Hate-Good. Lord Hate-Good was a despicable character—a liar, and he passed sentence on these two Christians, condemning both of them to death. In fact, he wanted them to be put to death immediately. He had no time for Christian or Faithful; no interest in their religion; no love for their God; no desire to spare their lives; and no sense of right or wrong. As his name indicates, he was a man who hated everything that was good and loved everything that was wrong. In Bunyan's story, Faithful was killed. In the providence of God, Christian was spared, and Lord Hate-Good's plans for him were foiled.

When I read of Lord Hate-Good and his evil ways and judgments and desires, I cannot help but think of Haman the Persian prime minister. He had a similar outlook towards the people of God. Remember, he was in a powerful position in the world's largest empire. He was almost as wealthy as the king himself. He had authority to make laws and have them signed into force.

He had a large family that gave him credibility in the eyes of others, and he was in constant contact with the king. Yet, none of that really satisfied him. There was something, or to be more accurate, someone, who vexed him and made him intensely angry. Haman could not get over the fact that Mordecai, a Jew, would not reverence him or respect him. That one thing filled him with indignation. It was constantly before him. When he received advice from his wife and friends that he should order gallows to be built and then ask the king's permission to hang Mordecai in the morning, it seemed like the perfect plan.

Haman had been invited to a banquet with the king and queen the next day. He felt that if he could get rid of Mordecai first, he could go into that banquet without a care in the world. So the gallows were made, and in Haman's mind Mordecai was dead.

That brings us to Esther 6. For early the next day Haman made his way to the king's court, and within minutes of arriving there he was immediately brought into the king's room. For a few moments Haman took centre stage. However, his life was about to a take a dramatic turn for the worse. This leads us to consider Esther 6:6-9:

> So Haman came in. And the king said unto him, What shall be done unto the man whom the king delighteth to honour? Now Haman thought in his heart, To whom would the king delight to do honour more than to myself? And Haman answered the king, For the man whom the king delighteth to honour, Let the royal apparel be brought which the king useth to wear, and the horse that the king rideth upon, and the crown royal which is set upon his head. And let this apparel and horse be delivered to the hand of one of the king's most noble princes, that they may array the man withal whom the king delighteth to honour, and bring him on horseback through the street of the city, and proclaim before him, Thus shall it be done to the man whom the king delighteth to honour.

It all looked good for Haman. But when in v. 10 the king essentially said, "Okay, hurry up, and do all of that to Mordecai the Jew that sits at the king's gate," Haman's life fell apart. The wretched man of Persia, who had deceived himself, was learning that he had not deceived God, and he was about to reap what he had sown.

Why is this important for us? Because there are many Hamans in this world. There are many sinners who think they are wise but are really fools. They think they have all the answers to life's great questions and that they can play fast and loose with gospel truths.

Many think the things of God do not really matter, and that life is all about now and what they can do to satisfy themselves. The tragedy is that while they go on in their sinful ways, it is the way of death and damnation. The sinner is going to fall. That is tragically illustrated for us in the life of Haman. Let us consider "The Fall of a Foolish Sinner." There are four parts to this unfolding drama that need closer attention:

THE SINNER'S CONTEMPT

It is hard to read the details of Esther 6 and not form the opinion that Haman was a shameless and despicable type of man. From the first time we meet him in Esther 3, we discover that he was full of his own importance. His high rank in the government of Persia was matched by his high estimation of himself. He was proud and self-centred. Haman's heart was full of idols; and the greatest idol was the idol of self. He worshipped himself and felt everyone else ought to worship him, too.

Haman's heart (like the heart of every sinner) was a wicked mix of idolatry, pride, rebellion, hardness, deceitfulness, evil thoughts, and ungodliness. There was nothing good in him. His heart was deceitful and desperately wicked. That wicked heart of his showed itself in a life that was full of contempt. Proverbs 23:7 tells us that "As a man thinketh in his heart so is he." In other words, out of his heart are the issues of life. Therefore, if the heart is hardened and defiant and still without redemption, then it follows that the life will reflect that.

Thomas Goodwin once said, "Self-love is king in unregenerate hearts." He added "Self is the most abominable principle that ever was." And so it proved in the case of Haman. This wicked man cared for nothing or no one but himself and his own interests, and as a result he held the things of God—and especially the law of God—in contempt.

When Haman left his home and made his way toward the outer court of the king's house in Esther 6:4, he had murder in his heart. "...Haman was come into the outward court of the king's house to speak unto the king to hang Mordecai on the gallows that he had made for him." There was only one thing on his mind that morning. When the verse says that he came to speak unto the king, we can be sure that he had rehearsed what he was going to say. This matter had filled his thoughts. He had consulted with friends. He had made arrangements for the gallows to be made, and the last thing he needed to do was speak with the king.

There was a progression in sin, here, and it all stemmed from the thoughts of his heart. Haman was planning to kill Mordecai. This was not after due process of law. It was not because Mordecai had been found guilty of a capital crime. Remember, Mordecai had served the king well and had exposed the crimes of others. He was not a renowned criminal who deserved to die. Rather, Haman was ready to kill this man because of the wickedness of his own heart.

He was angry with Mordecai, and that anger had festered and been nurtured so much so that Haman was ready to break the sixth commandment and put him to death. Of course, this is not the first time we discover murder in this man's heart. In Esther 3, he succeeded in having the king pass a law that every Jew living in Persia should be killed. That was a murderous plan. Haman lived this way. He had a problem with one Jew, so he decided to kill all the Jews. He did not seem to have a twinge of conscience about this.

Haman's heart was hardened. Therefore, he treated the law of God, the people of God, and the common grace of God with utter contempt.

Does that not sound familiar? The sinner's heart is often full of disdain for the things of God, so much so that he continues on his sinful way without a thought of the Lord. In Psalm 10:4, the psalmist said, "The wicked, through the pride of his countenance, will not seek after God: God is not in all his thoughts." What does that mean? It means he does not care to think of God.

Albert Barnes in his notes on this verse wrote as follows:

> The phrase "after God," is supplied by our translators. Something clearly is to be supplied, and it is plainly something relating to God—either that the wicked man will not seek after God in prayer, or that he will not inquire after the proofs of his existence and attributes; or that he will not seek after his favor, or that he will not endeavor to know the divine will. All this would be implied in seeking after God, and this is undoubtedly the state of mind that is referred to here. The sinner is unwilling, in any appropriate way, to acknowledge God.[10]

He holds God in contempt. Think on that. The sinner lives because God is gracious to him. He owes his very life—his next breath—to God. He enjoys the blessings God sends to him—his food, his strength, his ability to work and move and do things. But though he is dependent on God for everything, he thumbs his nose at God and sins as if God were not there. What happens when a sinner breaks the first commandment? What happens when he breaks the second commandment, or the third or the fourth or any of the commandments? He is showing his contempt for God. It is as if he is saying, "I will not obey Him, I do not care for Him, I will not honour Him, I do not serve Him...." He holds God and the things of God in utter contempt. Remember the words of Pharaoh in Exodus 5:2: "Who is the LORD, that I should obey his voice to let Israel go? I know not the LORD, neither will I let Israel go." Is that where you are right now? Are you living in defiance of God?

10   Albert Barnes, *Notes, Critical, Explanatory and Practical on the Book of Psalms* Vol 1, 89.

THE SINNER'S CONFIDENCE

Haman was full of self-belief and self-assurance. When he rose up early that morning and made his way to the royal court, he was absolutely sure that he had a perfect plan in place. I suspect he played the details over and over in his mind. He would have re-lived the days before: the invitation to the first banquet, the invitation to the second banquet, the anger he felt towards Mordecai, and then the suggestion from his wife and friends to have gallows made and the plan to kill Mordecai the next day. Then, the next morning had come. When Haman made his way to the palace, he was absolutely sure all was well. What could go wrong? How could it fail? Who could stop him? From v. 4 to v. 9 we find a man who was confident, composed, and certain. That comes very much to the fore in v. 6, when Ahasuerus asked, "What shall be done unto the man whom the king delighteth to honour?" Note the next few words: "Haman thought in his heart, To whom would the king delight to do honour more than to myself?" He thought in *his heart*.

It is as if he reasoned in his own heart, "I'm the most likely candidate for the king's honour. There is no one else like me. There is no one better than me. Who else would the king like to reward?" The man exudes confidence. Haman never entertained the idea that his little proud life could unravel at any time. He never imagined that things were moving towards his destruction. He never thought that he was about to face the king's wrath or about to be hanged on his own gallows. But he thought in his heart that all was well and that he was going to prosper even more.

That is why he answered the king as he did. The words of vv. 7-9 show just how confident he was. When he answered the king and thought the king was thinking of him, he set forth a plan that was excessive.

> And Haman answered the king, For the man whom the king delighteth to honour, Let the royal apparel be brought which the king *useth* to wear, and the horse that the king rideth upon, and the crown royal which is set

upon his head: And let this apparel and horse be delivered to the hand of one of the king's most noble princes, that they may array the man *withal* whom the king delighteth to honour, and bring him on horseback through the street of the city, and proclaim before him, Thus shall it be done to the man whom the king delighteth to honour.

Haman wanted all this honour. He was confident in his sin, confident in himself, and confident in his success. Is that not just like the sinner? The unregenerate man thinks he is practically invincible. He is confident in his own decision, ways, abilities, strength, wisdom, actions, and in his own opinions of himself. In Proverbs 1:29, 30 Solomon said, "For they that hated knowledge, and did not choose the fear of the LORD; they would none of my counsel: they despised all my reproof."

What would make a man do that? What would make a man refuse the Word of God and despise His correction? Self-confidence. The proud sinner feels he does not need God. He believes he is self-sufficient. His heart is full of self-assurance. "Why would God not like me? Why would God not accept me? Why would God not let me into heaven? Why would God not bless me throughout eternity?" They are confident that all is well with them! Are you like that? Like the rich farmer in Luke 12, do you think you have time to spare—many years ahead of you? Is that why you are rejecting the gospel? Be warned. For this chapter not only speaks of the sinner's contempt and the sinner's confidence but also of the sinner's confounding

THE SINNER'S CONFOUNDING

Pay close attention to v. 10. It is a remarkable text. This is one of the jaw-dropping moments in the book. The words and the order of the words and the suspense in that order are very important. Haman was happy until the very moment the king mentioned Mordecai, then added "the Jew" that sits at the gate. In that moment Haman was full of consternation. He was confounded. And I want you to see that it was a word from the king that confounded this foolish sinner. This was *unexpected,* for Haman never saw it coming. It was *unanswerable,* for he never spoke another word at this time. And it was *unchangeable,* for he had to go (v. 12). He went with his head covered like a prisoner being taken into prison and wanting to hide his face from the press. He could not bare the shame of it. His wretched life of dishonesty and pride and self-importance had suffered a blow from which it would never recover.

This reminds me of Matthew 22:11, 12: "And when the king came in to see the guests, he saw there a man which had not on a wedding garment: And he saith unto him, Friend, how camest thou in hither not having a wedding garment? And he was speechless."

If you are an unbeliever, the time will come when you will be confounded by the word of the King. All your sinful schemes, all your self-righteousness, all your selfish plans, all your animosity towards the Lord and His people, all your devious ways, all your self-confidence, all your vain ideas, all your pride, all your godless hopes—all these will start to crack and fall apart. You will not have one thing to say. This is a sobering, solemn truth.

THE SINNER'S COLLAPSE

The contrast between Haman's entrance to the palace and his exit from the palace could not have been more stark. His egotisic world had fallen apart. It was a monumental collapse of a man who thought he was invincible. There are two things that stand out from the closing verses of Esther 6. One relates to the loneliness of Haman. As he hasted to his home, mourning, he cut a very lonely figure. His head was covered and undoubtedly very heavy. And he was alone. Even when he returned home and his friends and family told him he could not now prevail, he must have felt deserted and desolated. Human support is fickle. In this case it was worthless. It will be a fearful thing when the sinner stands alone before God. He will have no support—and certainly no Saviour.

The other truth that stands out from these verses is the hopelessness of Haman. How those words, "Thou shalt not prevail against him, but thou shalt surely fall before him" must have stung him. The game he had played was over. The noose was tightening around him and he was on the verge of being dealt with in wrath. Haman was going to fall. Payday for him was just around the corner—for in under twenty-four hours, he would receive the wages for his sin.

These are solemn observations, however, true for all of that. The day will come when impenitent sinners will fall and perish in their sin. Their foot shall slide, and they will not be able to stand before God. They will be, as Jonathan Edwards once said, sinners in the hands of an angry God. Be warned—the wages of sin is death.

12

Exposed and Executed

And Esther said, The adversary and enemy is this wicked Haman. Then Haman was afraid before the king and the queen.

Esther 7:6

Esther 7 provides us with details of one of the most extraordinary banquets ever held in the history of the Persian Empire. The banquet in question was the second one to be held in the space of twenty-four hours. It had not been arranged to celebrate some notable victory in war or to announce a royal birth. Rather it had been set in place by Queen Esther because she had something very heavy and important upon her heart.

Back in Esther 4, when Esther had learned of a plot to kill her and all the other Jews living in the kingdom, she determined to break with royal etiquette and go in uninvited to the king and plead for her people.

So, in Esther 5, she asked the king to call Haman, and together with him come to a banquet that she had prepared. They accepted the invitation, and when Ahasuerus pressed her to make her request known and state her petition, Esther simply asked that both men would come the following day to another banquet.

But that night, strange things happened in Persia. The king could not sleep, and, in his restlessness (as mentioned earlier in chapter 10) he discovered that Mordecai had not been rewarded for a good deed he had done for the king some years earlier. During the same night, but in a different part of the capital city, Haman had ordered a set of gallows to be built so that he could hang Mordecai first thing the next morning.

Both men were thinking of Mordecai, but for completely different reasons. And when the morning came, the king spoke first and asked Haman what should be done to the man whom the king delights to honour. Haman, believing that the king was thinking of him, suggested that the man should be dressed in the royal robes, given the royal crown, placed on the royal horse, taken through the streets of the city, and announced as the man in whom the king delights. As far as Haman was concerned it was a done deal. Then the king dropped the bombshell and told Haman to do all of that to *Mordecai the Jew*.

I think it is fair to say that it was the worst morning of Haman's life. His plans were falling apart. He was humiliated and broken and ashamed all at the same time. When he finished leading Mordecai through the city, he went home and told his wife all that had happened. She was anything but comforting, for she essentially said, "You will not prevail against this man... it is really all over for you, Haman." As they were talking, the king's servants arrived and hurriedly took Haman to the second banquet.

This time the atmosphere was very different. For when the king said to Esther (for the third time in two days), "What is thy petition queen Esther? and it shall be granted thee: and what is thy request? and it shall be performed, even to the half of the kingdom," Esther began the speech of her life.

If you do a search for the top ten speeches in history, you will find words by prime ministers, presidents, and politicians of all shades of opinion. Some of those speeches have to do with war, slavery, or human rights. Some of the speeches were inspirational and all of them were influential. But I venture to say that not one of them was as important as Esther's speech during this second banquet in Persia.

There she was, a young queen telling her husband, the king, that a plot had been laid not only to kill her but to kill all her people. And when the king enquired of her, "Who has done such a thing?" she immediately said in the presence of Haman, "The adversary and enemy is this wicked Haman." It was the speech of her life. This was Esther's moment. This was why she had been chosen to be the queen. This was why she was accepted, even when she was not invited. This was why God had her where she was. She had come to the kingdom for such a time as this.

Her intervention at this point in history was marked with tremendous courage. Esther really stepped up to the mark. She had concealed her Jewishness up until this point; but now she clearly identified herself with the Lord's people. She might have been afraid, for fear in such circumstances is natural. But she was not ashamed to count herself among the Jews. She had said to Mordecai, "I go…and if I perish, I perish." She did not perish. But this took tremendous courage, and to name Haman as the adversary and wicked man that he was took courage too. I fear such courage is lacking among many of the Lord's people. Some have never really declared that they belong to Christ, and it is hard to tell where they stand. Not so with Esther.

Furthermore, her intervention was marked with great wisdom. Why did she ask for two banquets? Why did she not tell Ahasuerus what was on her heart immediately? By patiently waiting, she succeeded in obtaining a threefold promise from him that he would give her up to half of his kingdom. He was saying that he would give her whatever she asked for. He could hardly go back on his word now. This was a very good move on Esther's part.

Then note the words she used in v. 3: "Let my life be given me at my petition, and my people at my request." She put herself first. Why? Because Ahasuerus loved her, and if he thought that someone was trying to kill his wife, he would immediately move for her defence. Note also the terms in v. 4: "For we are sold, I and my people, to be destroyed, to be slain and to perish." Those were the exact words of the decree against the Jews (Esther 3). Esther was very wise in her approach to the matter. She had everything in place. And then when it came to the climax of her speech and the king said, "Who is he...?" She immediately said, "The adversary and enemy is this wicked Haman." Esther is to be commended for her intervention here. God was at work. But as is often the case, He was working through instruments, and this was Esther's moment.

It was a high point for her, but the lowest of low points for Haman. In fact, he never recovered from this. The night before, he had gallows built to hang Mordecai, but before the next night had come, he had been hanged on his own gallows. And it is that aspect of this chapter that I want us to focus on here. It really is an extension of what begins to emerge in chapter 6. The sin of this man is beginning to find him out, and now in this chapter Haman is humiliated and hanged. What do we learn? We learn that a sinner reaps what he sows. And while he may be sure of himself, he needs to be sure that his sin will find him out and that the wages of sin is death. Three words summarise these verses with that in mind.

DISCLOSURE

Esther's speech contains a precise account of all that was wrong with Haman. For weeks this man had walked around Shushan the palace thinking very highly of himself. As we have noticed in previous chapters, he was full of pride, self-importance, arrogance, and craft. He was a smooth talker, a man who believed in himself and felt that everything was under his control. He even succeeded in gaining the confidence of the king and managed to have a law of genocide passed against the Jews without giving all of the details. Haman was shrewd man—a sinful man—and for a time it seemed as if he was going to prosper. In Esther 7 he was eventually exposed.

When Esther spoke to the king during the second banquet, she made a full disclosure of who Haman really was and what Haman was really doing. According to v. 4, he had sold her and her people, so that they would be destroyed. Then, when Aha-suerus asked, "Who is he?" she said, in the words of v. 6, "The adversary and enemy is this wicked Haman." Those words were deliberate and significant.

The word "adversary" comes from two words which mean a man who is hostile, a man who persecutes. It is a word that implies hatred and great hostility, one who has the intention of injuring and persevering in his persecution. Then she used the word "enemy." That is a term that has the thought of anger or rage. It means to bind up in order to afflict or to oppress.

Esther also spoke of him as "this wicked Haman" or, as it could be rendered, "this wicked one Haman." All of those words were designed to show the king the truth about this man. The lon-ger she spoke, the more details she gave, and the more personal and precise she became, the focus moved from her to Haman. So there he was with nowhere to hide, nowhere to go, in the full glare of the truth of her statements, exposed for what he really was. Nothing was held back. This full disclosure falls into two categories:

Haman's conduct: By the time Esther was finished, she had dealt with the evil plans Haman had against her and her people. He was going to move against all the Jews across the 127 provinces of the Persian Empire and have them put to death. This man had put his hand to a law that broke the law of God. His conduct was extremely sinful. He neither loved God nor his neighbour as himself. He was guilty of murder in his heart. Haman lived an ungodly life. Esther exposed that.

Haman's character: When Esther said, "This wicked Haman," she came to the very heart of this man's ungodliness and wretch-edness. For sure, he had made wicked plans and was about to implement a wicked programme, but the reason for all of that was that he was a wicked man. If Jeremiah had lived at the same time, he would have said of him, "His heart is deceitful above all things and desperately wicked" (see Jeremiah 17:9) Haman's problems were not on the surface. Haman was not just a bad man on the outside. He was a wicked man through and through. It is interesting that the word "wicked" is used in Genesis 6:5, where we read of the people in days of Noah: "And GOD saw that the wickedness of man was great in the earth, and that every imagination of the thoughts of his heart was only evil [or wicked] continually."

This is man in his natural state. He is not only a sinner by practice; he is a sinner by nature. There is an inherent wickedness in the heart. This is what Paul emphasised in such precise detail in Romans 3 when he said, "There is none righteous, no, not one: There is none that understandeth, there is none that seeketh after God. They are all gone out of the way, they are together become unprofitable; there is none that doeth good, no, not one.... There is no fear of God before their eyes." This is not so much about *what the sinner does,* as it is about *who the sinner is.* He is sinful in his character.

This is something that is often forgotten. There is a tendency for a person to think, "As long as I do not act a certain way, or commit certain crimes, as long as I do not say or do what others say or do...then I will meet God's standard." Not so. We are not sinners because we sin; we sin because we are sinners. There is something fundamentally wrong, something that goes deeper than our words or actions; it goes right to our heart. There is wickedness there. A person may try to cover that by living a certain way and giving the impression all is well. However, the Scriptures disclose this deep-seated problem. God knows the existence, extent, and evidence of our sinfulness.

Haman was wicked from his heart out. So is every sinner, and we must face up to that. There is no hiding it. This book reveals it. God exposes it.

DREAD

Until this point in the book Haman had been confident, composed, and certain of his plans. He felt himself to be the king in his own little world. However, in Esther 7:6, when Esther revealed his wickedness and showed the king what he really was, we are told, "Then Haman was afraid before the king and the queen." The word "afraid" means to be terrified. His entire outlook changed. He knew his game was up. He knew his sinfulness was open for these people to see. He knew the king would not tolerate him for another moment, and he was terrified. Dread laid hold of this man in a way it had never laid hold of him before. There are three parts to this:

HE WAS UNABLE TO MOUNT ANY KIND OF DEFENCE BEFORE THE KING.

Haman was afraid before the king, but he never spoke to the king. There was no attempt to justify his actions; no attempt to reason that the king had been part of all this (after all, he had signed the plan into law). There was no effort to excuse himself. Haman was speechless. He was so overcome with terror that not one word would have prevailed with the king.

HE WAS AFRAID TO DIE.

Verse 7 is one of many dramatic moments in the chapter. The king had repeatedly asked Esther to make her request and petition known. At the second banquet she had asked for her life and the life of her people to be spared, and she named Haman as the murderer. Now he was pleading for his life. He did not want to die. He was happy for Mordecai to hang from the gallows, happy for the Jews to be put to death on the thirteenth day of the twelfth month. He was happy for the streets of Persia to run red with their blood; but he was afraid to die himself.

HE THREW HIMSELF UPON THE MERCY OF THE QUEEN.

Is it not interesting that he did not call upon the Lord to have mercy upon him. There is not a word of repentance. His fear was for the consequences of his sin, but not for the sin itself.

Here was a man whose life of sin, rebellion, hatred, and bitterness had caught up with him. He was staring judgment in the face, and it had filled him with terror. According to v. 7, he knew that there was evil determined against him by the king, and he was absolutely helpless. What does that show us? There will come a day when the sinner who has boldly defied God will tremble before God, and he will not be bold in that last day. The Lord states: "I also will laugh at your calamity; I will mock when your fear cometh; When your fear cometh as desolation, and your destruction cometh as a whirlwind; when distress and anguish cometh upon you" (Proverbs 1:26, 27). Solomon confirmed: "The fear of the wicked it shall come upon him" (Proverbs 10:24). That day will come when unbelievers will have no defence before God, and all their pleading will be in vain.

<h2 style="text-align:center">DEATH</h2>

Consider the record of Esther 7:8-10. What was happening? The king went out to the garden in a rage. Why? Why did he not call for Haman to be taken and killed at once? Was it because he knew that he was implicated in this also? He had signed this thing into law. He had given Haman the royal ring to seal this matter; therefore, there must have been a sense of responsibility. Certainly he was vexed with Haman, and when he returned, he found him pleading with Esther. We learn in v. 8 that this enraged the king more, and he cried out, "Will he force the queen also...?" It seems that Ahasuerus used this as the reason to call for Haman's death. In some ways he made it convenient for himself by speaking this way of Haman. Just then—and this proves to be perfect timing again—Harbonah mentioned the gallows that Haman had made. His face was covered, and he was taken off and hanged.

The Scriptures make it is clear in numerous places that the sinner who hardens himself against God cannot prosper. There is an aftermath to sin and God will bring the sinner to account. The following texts prove the point beyond all shadow of doubt. Numbers 32:23: "Be sure your sin will find you out." Galatians 6:7, "Be not deceived; God is not mocked: for whatsoever a man soweth, that shall he also reap." Job 5:12-14: "He disappointeth the devices of the crafty, so that their hands cannot perform their enterprise. He taketh the wise in their own craftiness: and the counsel of the froward is carried headlong. They meet with darkness in the daytime, and grope in the noonday as in the night."

Sinful man sets his course and believes he is right and will be rewarded. What he fails to note is that the way that seems right to man is the way of death. The ungodly cannot prosper eternally. God cannot—and will not—be fooled. Haman was a self-deceived man. He did not deceive God. A day of reckoning came for him. This is a sobering observation for all who are yet in their sin. Each person is accountable to God, and God will not overlook our sin against Him. Therefore, the gospel commands each one to turn from sin, and believe in the Lord Jesus Christ. There is no other Saviour and no other way of salvation.

For Such a Time as This

13

A Good Day for God's People

*And in every province, and in every city, whithersoever
the king's commandment and his decree came, the Jews
had joy and gladness, a feast and a good day. And many
of the people of the land became Jews; for the fear of the
Jews fell upon them.*

Esther 8:17

The closing part of Esther 7 records the sudden and very dramatic hanging of Haman the prime minister of Persia. In an extraordinary turn of events—over a thirty-six-hour period—Haman went from being one of the most powerful men in the kingdom to being one of the most powerless. Prior to this most unusual episode, he had been at the centre of a plot to destroy all the Jews living in Persia. It looked as if his plan was destined to succeed.

Haman had secured the support of the king. He had sent out letters outlining the plan. He had gallows built and was about to hang Mordecai the Jew. Everything looked to be in place. However, Haman had not reckoned on God. He had no idea that in God's providence, Esther, the queen of Persia and herself a Jew, was about to expose him as a wicked and deceitful enemy. When she dropped that bombshell, recorded in Esther 7, the king wasted no time in ordering that Haman should be hanged on his own gallows.

While Esther 7 does not provide us with any of the details, I think it is reasonable to suggest that the sudden public execution of the prime minster must have sent shock waves throughout the entire empire. This had happened so quickly. One day he was walking through the palace as a prominent, trusted, and favoured member of the royal household, but within hours the same man was judged to have committed a crime and paid for that with his life. It was certainly a dramatic end to a dramatic chapter. Let us reinforce some of the most important lessons from the sudden death of Haman.

THERE IS JUST A STEP BETWEEN ANY MAN AND DEATH.

When Haman arose that morning and made his way to the palace, he never expected that this was going to be his last day on earth. He would never have given a second thought to the possibility that he was hours away from his own death. But before that day was over, he had been hanged on his own gallows. There was just a step between him and death, and he was not ready for it. We should not let that lesson be lost on us. Solomon urges, "Boast not thyself of tomorrow, for thou knowest not what a day may bring forth" (Proverbs 27:1). Death could come at any moment—and after death, the judgment.

OUR SIN WILL FIND US OUT.

Haman's plan against the Jews had sin written all over it. He had no good reason to act against them in this way. His pride and self-idolatry and murderous intent all flowed from his wicked heart. And while his plan to massacre the Jews was approved by the king, it was never approved by God. It was a sinful plan; and in Esther 7, it was exposed and Haman was uncovered for what he really was. His sin had found him out. That is a universal law. God knows the full extent of sin in the human heart: the thoughts, the actions, and the words of all people. And while some refuse to repent and try to cover them up, the day will come when every sin will be laid bare and every sinner exposed.

RETRIBUTION WILL BE JUST AND FAIR.

Haman had shown no mercy towards Mordecai and no mercy towards the Jews. He was set on slaughtering every one of them in the kingdom. He had no pity, no compassion, and no sympathy for any of God's people. When it came to his time of judgment, he discovered that there was no mercy. He pleaded for it. In one of the most ironic scenes in the book, he fell before Esther and pleaded for his life. However, one who acted without mercy was judged without mercy. The New Testament addresses this very issue with these words: "For he shall have judgment without mercy, that hath shewed no mercy" (James 2:13). Are you without mercy? Do you live without love towards God or faith in Jesus Christ? Do you go on in your sin? If so, you will be judged accordingly.

GOD OVERRULES THE WICKEDNESS OF MAN FOR HIS OWN GLORY.

This is the underlying theme in the book. God is overruling. God is in control. He will be glorified—glorified in the salvation of His people and in the destruction of His enemies. He will make His Name known, and every tongue will confess that Jesus Christ is Lord. These are important lessons from the dramatic end of Esther 7.

But it would be entirely wrong to think that the events at the end of Esther 7 mark the last of the drama in Persia. Haman's *life* had been taken, but Haman's *law* against the Jews was still in place. Therefore, things were still on track for a terrible massacre to take place on the thirteenth day of the twelfth month. However, as God had overruled in the matter of this wicked man, so He was going to overrule in the matter of this wicked plan. That is what forms the detail in this chapter. Esther 8 is a chapter that records a good day for God's people, and it is easily divided into four parts.

A Great Reversal

Up to this point in the book of Esther, Haman had appeared as the wealthy, influential, successful, and thriving prime minister. Under Ahasuerus he had risen to a prominent position in the kingdom. He exuded confidence and boldness. He was a man who had gone to the top of the career ladder and was flourishing in his role in the kingdom. Although his life was full of horrible sin, Haman seemed to have it all. He had houses and land and silver and gold. More than that, he was in the inner circle of the king's friends and had the ability to influence laws throughout the Persian Empire. He was an ungodly man who always seemed to be prospering.

On the other hand, Mordecai and Esther and the millions of other Jews were on the verge of extinction. If Haman had had his way, the Jews would have been downtrodden and destroyed. The contrast was phenomenal. An ungodly man was prospering, while God's covenant people were on the edge of disaster.

But note the great turnaround that is recorded in Esther 7:10 and Esther 8:1: "So they hanged Haman on the gallows that he had prepared for Mordecai." "On that day did the king Ahasuerus give the house of Haman the Jews' enemy unto Esther the queen." The apparent prosperity of Haman did not last. He lost everything; whereas the poor people of God were delivered and enriched. Observe also the words of v. 2: "The king took off his ring, which he had taken from Haman, and gave it unto Mordecai. And Esther set Mordecai over the house of Haman." What a reversal! Not only did Haman lose his land and his houses and his riches, but his avowed enemy was placed over them. There are several lessons here.

THE PROSPERITY OF THE WICKED IS TEMPORARY.

Evil men might seem to prosper, but their prosperity will not last. This was the very issue that Asaph wrestled with in Psalm 73: 2, 3: "But as for me, my feet were almost gone; my steps had well nigh slipped. For I was envious at the foolish, when I saw the prosperity of the wicked." He went on to explain that when he looked at the wicked, he saw men who were strong, who never seemed to be in trouble, and who seemed to get their own way. He saw those who continued in their sinful ways, apparently without any problem. They appeared to get on in life and never suffered like he was suffering. He began to envy them.

He summarized it thus in v. 12: "Behold, these are the ungodly, who prosper in the world; they increase in riches." We know people like that: the ungodly celebrities; politicians; work colleagues who have no time for God and no time for His people. Yet they get on in life. It can be very disturbing. But Asaph did not end there. He said in vv. 16-19, "When I thought to know this, it was too painful for me; Until I went into the sanctuary of God; then understood I their end. Surely thou didst set them in slippery places: thou castedst them down into destruction. How are they brought into desolation, as in a moment! They are utterly consumed with terrors." Do not be envious of the wicked, for their prosperity will be short lived. Their feet will slip in God's time.

THE LORD WILL HONOUR THOSE WHO HONOUR HIM.

Esther and Mordecai were faithful in this matter: Mordecai refused to give worship to Haman that should only be given to God. Esther approached her entrance in before the king, trusting that God had brought her to the kingdom for such a time as this. Though they were not all they should have been in Persia, they did honour the Lord, and He honoured them. This principle is confirmed in another Old Testament setting: "I said indeed that thy house, and the house of thy father, should walk before me for ever: but now the LORD saith, Be it far from me; for them that honour me I will honour, and they that despise me shall be lightly esteemed" (1 Samuel 2:30). The world will not honour God's people for their godliness; but the Lord will.

LET US NOT JUDGE A MATTER BEFORE ITS END.

If you had been a Jew living in Persia at this time, you might have thought that all was doomed. Haman's law had been passed. The king's seal was upon it. It was the law of the Persian Empire. It could not be revoked. Haman was going to win the day. However, not everything ends as it begins. Things changed between Esther 7 and Esther 8. The antagonist—the adversary—the enemy was dead, and his intended victim Mordecai was not only alive, but had been set over his house. Are you in despair? The end is not yet, and the best is yet to be. What did William Cowper say?

> *God's purposes will ripen fast,*
> *Unfolding every hour;*
> *The bud may have a bitter taste,*
> *But sweet will be the flower.*[11]

There is a great reversal here. Why? Because God is on the throne. Believer, whatever situation you are in today, trust Him to do His perfect will and bring all things together for your good and His great glory.

A Great Request

Although Haman was dead, Haman's decree against the Jews was still in place. So for the second time in the space of a few hours Esther approached the king again and began to plead for her people. The details are in Esther 8:3-6:

> And Esther spake yet again before the king, and fell down at his feet, and besought him with tears to put away the mischief of Haman the Agagite, and his device that he had devised against the Jews. Then the king held out the golden sceptre toward Esther. So Esther arose, and stood before the king, And said, If it please the king, and if I have found favour in his sight, and the thing seem right before the king, and I be pleasing in his eyes, let it be written to reverse the letters devised by Haman the son of Hammedatha the Agagite, which he wrote to destroy the Jews which *are* in all the king's provinces: For how can I endure to see the evil that shall come unto my people? or how can I endure to see the destruction of my kindred?

Note certain things here. *Her position:* She fell at the king's

---

11   William Cowper, *God Moves in a Mysterious Way*

feet. That was a place of humility and submission. *Her passion:* She besought him with tears. This is the only time in the book that we read of Esther crying. This was not mere emotion. This was earnest crying for her people. *Her petition:* In v. 3 she asked the king, "to put away the mischief (an alternative translation would be *wickedness* or *evil*) of Haman the Agagite and his device that he had devised against the Jews."

She was pleading for the life of her people. This was the one thing that was on her heart. She did *not* request the house of Haman be given to her. She did *not* ask for his wealth to be transferred to her account. She did *not* ask for Mordecai to be exalted. She was asking for the lives of her people to be spared. The plea that she made reached its climax in v. 6 when she said, "For how can I endure to see the evil that shall come unto my people? Or how can I endure to see the destruction of my kindred?" Esther the queen is Esther the intercessor. In chapter 5, she had made a request to the king and asked him to come to the banquet, but this request was even greater. She could not bear the thought that her people, her fellow Jews, were going to die. She was genuinely moved at their plight.

In Romans 9:1-3, Paul wrote: "I say the truth in Christ, I lie not, my conscience also bearing me witness in the Holy Ghost, That I have great heaviness and continual sorrow in my heart. For I could wish that myself were accursed from Christ for my brethren, my kinsmen according to the flesh." Understand Paul at this point in his life. He was passionate about the salvation of his fellow Jews. There was a strong attachment between him and them, and therefore he spoke in the strongest possible terms about their deliverance. In this sense, Esther and Paul were the same. Surely, we should display a similar burden for the souls of men and women around us.

We live in a dying world, one where sinners are under the wrath and condemnation of God. The king's law is against them. If the divine law follows it course, and under God it must, then unless our friends and family have Christ as their Saviour, they will be destroyed and doomed to an eternity in hell for ever. It was a serious time for the Jews living in Persia. However, that was nothing in comparison to the seriousness of the situation facing a soul outside of Christ. Christian parents should pray for their children. We must go to the Lord with passionate prayer and beseech Him on their behalf.

There is another dimension here also. Esther was acting as an advocate for the Jews. Christ is our great Advocate. We have an adversary who tries to defeat us, but Christ prays for us. He intervenes on our behalf. He stands up for us. He pleads our case. By the merit of His blood and the victory of His death and resurrection, we are safe and secure. There are many pictures of intercession in this book. Let us look beyond Esther and fill our minds with thoughts of Christ pleading with prevailing prayers for His people.

A Great Ruling

When Esther finished making her plea to Ahasuerus, all eyes were fixed upon the king. What would he do? What could he do? What was his next step? The answer to those questions lies in the words of vv. 7-14. To summarise those words: Ahasuerus recognised that the initial decree set in place by Haman to slaughter all the Jews could not be changed. It was one of the reckless laws of the Medes and Persians, and even bad laws could not be reversed. He was in a dilemma. The law had been passed and could not be revoked. So he gave Mordecai permission to write another law and seal it with the king's ring. This would give the Jews permission to defend themselves against any who would attack them on the thirteenth day of the twelfth month.

Consider the language in v. 11: "Wherein the king granted the Jews which were in every city to gather themselves together, and to stand for their life, to destroy, to slay, and to cause to perish, all the power of the people and province that would assault them, both little ones and women and to take the spoil of them for a prey." The Jews had the right to self defence. Some commentators believe it went beyond self defence and allowed them to avenge themselves of their enemies. They were also permitted to take the spoils of war for themselves. This was the means whereby the Jews could be spared from the slaughter that was set against them. This was an imperfect plan, but under God it led to victory.

There are certain things here that correspond to the fact that there is a way whereby sinners condemned to death can be saved. Let us think of these particular details:

THIS WAY OF SALVATION RESTED ON THE AUTHORITY AND FAVOUR OF THE KING.

Only Ahasuerus could do what needed to be done, and it was when he showed favour to Esther that his ruling was given. The salvation of the sinner rests on the grace and power of God. Salvation is not something we can do for ourselves. Salvation is of the Lord. Only God can save.

THIS WAY OF SALVATION WAS ENACTED BY ONE WHO HAD BEEN EXALTED BY THE KING.

Mordecai is a leading figure in all of this. That much is clear from the words of v. 9 and v. 15. This was the same man who in Esther 4 was seen clothed in sackcloth and ashes, but now he was in royal robes. He was the man with whom the king was well pleased. Our salvation has been enacted by our Lord and Saviour, Jesus Christ, who is the exalted and well-beloved Son of God.

THIS WAY OF SALVATION WAS CONVEYED TO ALL THROUGHOUT THE EMPIRE.

Esther 8:13, 14 confirm that while the first law had been signed in the first month and this one in the third month, there were still several months before the proposed date of execution. This space of time was an opportunity for messages to be conveyed throughout the nation. It would have to be done with a sense of urgency. Time was of the essence if the opportunity was to be acted upon properly. In a parallel analogy, the gospel is to be spread with urgency. Time is short, and sinners must seek Christ while there is time and while He is near.

THIS WAY OF SALVATION WAS APPOINTED AND APPROVED.

It was sealed with the king's seal. It should be noted that there was only one way whereby the Jews could be spared. There is, of course, only one way sinners facing God's wrath can be delivered from certain judgment. That one way rests in the finished work of Christ. He has died as the Substitute. He offered Himself, without spot to God, thus purchasing eternal redemption for all who will trust in Him. God's salvation is sure and eternal.

A GREAT REJOICING

This brings me to the final verses in chapter 8. Even a cursory glance at these words will assure us that things were different. In Esther 4:3, four key words appear: "mourning, fasting, weeping, and wailing." These verses in Esther 8 also contain four key words—altogether different words—"light, gladness, joy, and honour."

The proposed deliverance of the Jews was an occasion for great joy. As v. 17 remarks, it was a "good day."

The gospel is good news for sinners and brings them into good blessing. There is no better or happier day in the life of an individual, than the day of such a person's deliverance from condemnation, through faith in Jesus Christ.

George Wade Robinson captured the thought of joy in the Christian's life with the words

Loved with everlasting love,
Led by grace that love to know;
Spirit, breathing from above,
Thou hast taught me it is so!
Oh, this full and perfect peace!
Oh, this transport all divine!
In a love which cannot cease,
I am His, and He is mine;
In a love which cannot cease,
I am His, and He is mine.

Heav'n above is softer blue,
Earth around is sweeter green!
Something lives in ev'ry hue
Christless eyes have never seen:
Birds with gladder songs o'erflow,
Flow'rs with deeper beauties shine,

Since I know, as now I know,
I am His, and He is mine;
Since I know, as now I know,
I am His, and He is mine.

Things that once were wild alarms
Cannot now disturb my rest;
Closed in everlasting arms,
Pillowed on the loving breast.
Oh, to lie forever here,
Doubt, and care, and self resign,
While He whispers in my ear,
I am His, and He is mine;
While He whispers in my ear,
I am His, and He is mine.

His forever, only His;
Who the Lord and me shall part?
Ah, with what a rest of bliss
Christ can fill the loving heart!
Heav'n and earth may fade and flee,
Firstborn light in gloom decline;
But while God and I shall be,
I am His, and He is mine;
But while God and I shall be,
I am His, and He is mine.

14

Victory for God's People

And all the rulers of the provinces, and the lieutenants,
and the deputies, and officers of the king, helped the
Jews; because the fear of Mordecai fell upon them.

Esther 9:3

For the major part of the book of Esther, a terrible threat hung over the existence of the Jews living throughout the Persian Empire. In chapter 3, Haman the prime minister plotted a massacre that would have wiped out the entire Jewish population.

As we have already considered, he was very particular with the terms of this plot. He wanted to destroy, to kill, and to cause to perish all Jews, both young and old, little children and women in one day. Those phrases are very significant. They speak of annihilation—not one Jew was to be spared. Every one of them, from the youngest to the oldest, was to be put to death.

Haman was not only particular with the terms of the plot; he was also particular with the timing of the plot. For as Esther 3 explains, he cast lots to determine the exact date that this massacre should take place. In the providence of God, the lot fell on the thirteenth day of Adar, which was the twelfth month. This was in the providence of God because it gave the Jews at least several months to prepare.

Although Haman's plan was extremely unjust and based on a foundation of pride and selfish ambition, he succeeded in having the king sign his proposals into law. That might not seem significant in western nations in the twenty-first century, for in our day laws can be scrutinized and checked, and legislation can be overthrown if needs be. If a bad law is made it can be revoked. That was not the case in the days of Esther. The Persians had a law that meant no law could be rescinded. So when Haman succeeded in obtaining the king's approval for his massacre of the Jews, it seemed that they were destined to be destroyed.

Between Esther 3 and the end of Esther 8, two very notable things took place: One was: *The sudden execution of Haman.* When Mordecai the Jew learned of this heinous plan to kill the Jews, he persuaded Queen Esther to go into the king and expose Haman as a wicked man. When she did, the king acted immediately and ordered that Haman should be put to death on the gallows he had built for Mordecai.

But his law was still in place. And that brings us to the second very notable thing: *The passing of another law allowing the Jews to defend themselves.* As King Ahasuerus could not set the decree permitting the execution of the Jews to the side, he established another law giving the Jews in Persia the right to resist any attack upon them. The exact terms of that law are spelled out in the words of Esther 8:11: "The king granted the Jews which were in every city to gather themselves together, and to stand for their life, to slay, and to cause to perish, all the power of the people and province that would assault them, both little ones and women, and to take the spoil of them for a prey." They had the right to act against those who would act against them.

All of this was leading up to the thirteenth day of the month Adar. I do not think it takes too much imagination to work through the tension that must have been rising throughout the empire as that date approached. Thousands of Gentiles were

determined to strike hard against the Jews. They were protected by law. They had months to prepare. They had listened to
the lies of Haman, and they were ready to destroy the Jewish
people. They were planning a holocaust against the Lord's chosen people, and their sights were set on that thirteenth day of
Adar. That would be the climax. That would be the Jews' final
day.

However, at the same time, the Jews were looking to the same
day and determined to defend themselves against all comers.
They, too, were protected by law. Clearly this was going to be a
pivotal day in the history of Persia and in the history of the Jews.

When the day arrived, the tables were turned on the Persians,
and the Jews entered into a time of glorious victory which is com-
memorated by Jews across the world to this day.

The theme of victory for God's people is written all over this
chapter. While thousands of their enemies were killed, there is
no record of any Jewish life being lost. Instead of the thirteenth
day of Adar being a day of destruction, it became a day of deliverance. The conflict that is recorded in these verses was followed
by celebration. The entire situation was reversed. God's purpose
was accomplished for His threatened people.

In a sense, we get a glimpse of the victory that God's people
can and ultimately will experience in a world that is horribly
set against them. Let us not forget that we are in a world that
is hostile and aggressive towards the things of God. We only
have to look around, and we see Christians being persecuted,
the laws of God being broken, and the gospel being despised.
Many are seeking the destruction of God's people. Nevertheless, God's people will know victory. Christ's church cannot be
overthrown.

THE REALITY OF THIS VICTORY

It is clear from the words of Esther 9:1 that the Jews' enemies con-
fidently anticipated their destruction. Note that phrase, "they
hoped to have power over them." These words signify that they
were sure they would have the mastery of them. These enemies
believed that they would win the day. They knew that Haman

had been executed; they knew that Queen Esther was a Jew and King Ahasuerus had listened to her; and they knew that there was a law permitting the Jews to defend themselves. They really should have read the warning signs. But such was their arrogance and pride that they thought they could fight against God and His people and still win. Nothing could have been further from the truth. The victory did not belong to them; it belonged to the Jews.

THIS VICTORY WAS ENJOYED BY A PEOPLE WHO RESOLVED TO FIGHT.

Esther 9:2 reveals that there was a sense of purpose and determination among the Jews at this time. The individual families all came together. They recognised that there was safety in unity. Had they acted separately, each family doing its own thing, they would have been an easy prey to their enemies. So they came together into their various cities and determined to resist their enemies. Verse 5 explains their mode of operation. This was self-defence; but that self-defence most likely and appropriately included preemptive strikes. The Jews acted as soldiers. They were not afraid to take up the sword and use it. They were not pacifists. In fact, in v. 13 Esther asked the king for an extension so that the war could continue. They understood that to win this struggle, they had to engage in the struggle.

Could it be that truth has been lost on the church in the twenty-first century? Sin often goes unchallenged. Heresy and apostasy are excused. Worldliness is explained in terms of Christian liberty. The church of Christ has been hampered by the religious equivalent of political correctness. And so the church stands for nothing. Yet we are commanded to fight! God has told us to stand against the wiles of the devil. Part of Christian living is to resist the enemy of our souls and to fight the good fight of faith. May God steel us for the battle.

THIS VICTORY CAME WHEN HEARTS WERE CHANGED TOWARDS GOD'S PEOPLE.

Verse 3 records that "all the rulers of the provinces, and the lieutenants and the deputies, and officers of the king, helped the Jews." What does that mean? It means the Jews found favour in the sight of these people. These people recognised the position Mordecai had in the kingdom, and their hearts were turned to help God's people. Is it not strange that sometimes God does that? He moves the hearts of men, even ungodly men, so that they act in favour of God's people. Solomon grasped that and said, "When a man's ways please the LORD, he maketh even his enemies to be at peace with him" (Proverbs 16:7). We might have expected these men to stand *against* the Jews; but they stood *with* them. Is that not what happened in the case of Nehemiah? The ungodly king favoured him as he went to rebuild the walls of Jerusalem. God can turn the hearts of ungodly men to favour His people.

THIS VICTORY WAS REALISED THROUGH THE DIRECT INTERVENTION OF GOD.

Consider the double reference to fear being upon the people in v. 2: "The fear of them fell upon all people." "The fear of Mordecai fell upon them." That raises a number of questions. Where did this fear fall from? What was it a fear of? Why did it come at this time? Who was behind this fear? The answer to those questions points to God. There is no other explanation for this other than to say God caused His fear to fall upon these people.

Has God not done that before? In Joshua 2:9, Rahab said to the two spies: "I know that the LORD hath given you the land, and that your terror is fallen upon us, and that all the inhabitants of the land faint because of you." Similarly, we read in Joshua 5:1, "And it came to pass, when all the kings of the Amorites, which were on the side of Jordan westward, and all the kings of the Canaanites, which were by the sea, heard that the LORD had dried up the waters of Jordan from before the children of Israel, until we were passed over, that their heart melted, neither was there spirit in them anymore, because of the children of Israel." This was the powerful intervention of God in the affairs of men so that His people would have the victory. He instilled fear into the hearts of others to protect and preserve His own people. God was fighting with and for His people. He still does.

THIS VICTORY WAS IN ACCORDANCE WITH GOD'S WILL.

Note the details in vv. 5-10. The ten sons of Haman the Agagite were put to death. That is important because of certain events that took place hundreds of years earlier. In 1 Samuel 15, Saul was told to destroy Agag and all the Amalekites. He failed, and as a result of that failure Haman eventually appeared and brought havoc to God's people. So the complete destruction of Haman and his sons testified to the eventual completion of that divine decree. This victory was in accordance with God's will.

THIS VICTORY WAS COMPREHENSIVE.

According to vv. 6, 15, and 16, almost 76,000 Persians died (800 in the capital city and 75,000 in the remainder of the Empire), but it seems that not one Jewish life was lost.

If we learn nothing else from this account, let us learn that God will preserve His own people. It was impossible for these Jews to be destroyed because God was for them. God had a purpose for the Jews. And of course, when we view this in the light of the church of Christ, we learn the same truth. We are despised, but Christ will build His church. Every believer should take comfort from this. Consider those men hanged on a tree; they were defeated. However, when Christ was hanged on the tree, He defeated Satan. He bruised the serpent's head and secured the ultimate victory for His people. We are in a hostile world, and that hostility is going to increase. Satan is busy, and wicked men are becoming worse and worse. We are in a battle. Notwithstanding the power and plan of Satan, our enemy, God is for us and Christ has died for us. Therefore, we are on the winning side. He will either save or destroy His enemies, and He will bring His people to enjoy a glorious victory. The end is not yet; but the victory is sure.

THE RESTRAINT IN THE VICTORY

There is a statement that is repeated three times in this chapter. Therefore it must be of great significance. It is found at the end of vv. 10, 15 and 16: "On the spoil or the prey they laid not their hand." In other words, the Jews did not take the spoils of war. According to Esther 8:11, they had right to take the spoil, but they chose not to. They exercised restraint in this matter. Why is that important? There are two reasons:

IT ADDRESSES THE ISSUE OF THEIR MOTIVES.

The reason why the Jews defended themselves so ably and so successfully was not for financial gain. They had no desire to amass wealth for themselves. Their aim was not driven by a desire for possessions. Their priority was their well-being, not their wealth. That tells me a whole lot about the mindset of these people; they were not living for earthly gain.

Matthew Henry said that they refused to take the spoil "that they might make it appear that they aimed at nothing but their own preservation, and used their interest at court for the saving of their lives, not for the raising of their estates."

Abraham showed a similar spirit when he returned from the war with Chedorlaomer the king of Elam in Genesis 14. Following his victory, the king of Sodom met him and offered him the spoils of war. Although Abraham was already a rich man, he could have become even richer. However, he responded to the king in the words of Genesis 14:22, 23: "I have lift up mine hand unto the LORD, the most high God, the possessor of heaven and earth, That I will not take from a thread even to a shoe-latchet, and that I will not take any thing that is thine, lest thou shouldest say, I have made Abram rich." He did not live for these things and did not want to give any occasion of praise or glory to the world. The Jews in Persia were the same. Their battle was not for personal gain.

Is there not a timely lesson for us? Are we not tempted sometimes to focus more on temporal things than we are on eternal things? We set about to gather up the things of this world. We put more emphasis on and more effort towards our possessions. Possessions in themselves are not wrong; we need them. The problem comes when we live for them, when we make too much of them, when we think more highly of them than we do of the Lord. If and when that happens, we fall into the snare of making idols out of them. According to Matthew 6:19-21 our treasure is to be in heaven! We ought to live with an eye to eternal wealth and living for Christ. Where are your priorities? What motivates you?

The law signed in Esther 8:11 permitted them to destroy the families of their enemies, even the little ones and the women. It seems from the narrative that the Jews did not do that. The language of the text indicates that they killed none but those who came against them; and therefore they did not take the spoil, but left it to the women and little ones, whom they spared. They did not kill them with the sword and would not kill them by starving them. It has been stated: "Herein they acted with a consideration and compassion well worthy of imitation."

While there were people in Persia who were not going to show any Jew any mercy, the Jews did not respond in kind; they did not take the spoils of war and therefore they did not inflict additional injury or hurt to the people.

Living for Christ and standing up for the gospel does not mean we have to behave in an ungodly way. Sadly, that happens sometimes. As the believer engages in spiritual warfare, resisting sin and earnestly contending for the faith, he must not dismiss the instructions from Scripture regarding his manner and motive. Strength and meekness go hand in hand. We ought to be gracious while being faithful. We can be marked with conviction and compassion at the one time. It is possible—indeed, essential—to hate sin, but also reach out to sinners and seek to win them to Christ. Our Lord Jesus is our great example. He was true, faithful, and stedfast, but also full of grace and truth. We must endeavour to speak the truth in love.

THE REMEMBRANCE OF THE VICTORY

If my calculations are correct, this is the eighth feast in the book of Esther. Eight is often described as the number of a new beginning. In this case, it certainly marked a new beginning in Persia for the Jews.

A careful consideration of vv. 17-28 will reveal that the victory God had given was celebrated with a great feast. It was a feast marked with praise, which involved all the people, and which is to be remembered permanently. The Jews still remember Purim. It is a happy holiday, which involes the reading of Esther and a time of feasting. On occasions, the name of Haman is written on the soles of the shoes and then the wearer jumps up and down, signifying the overthrow of the ancient enemy.

It is right for God's people to remember God's work on their behalf. To forget history is to forget the wonderful works and providences of God. If we fail to remember, we will fail to trust Him in present or future trials. Psalm 78 lays great emphasis on teaching our children the works of God. Such teaching is to be accompanied with the prayer that our offspring will put their trust in God also.

Above a general remembrance of God's grace, the Christian is commanded to remember the Lord and His atoning work. It is not without significance that Christ instituted what we know as the Lord's Supper or Lord's Table. Remembrance lies at the heart of that feast. Christ said, "This do in remembrance of me." The sad inference is that we are prone to forget Him. The provision of the communion feast is a gracious token of the Lord's mercy. When He instituted this, He remembered us; when we celebrate it, we remember Him.

Forgetting Christ—and the innumberable blessing Christians have in Him—is a sin to be avoided at all times and at all costs. Christ has gained the greatest victory of all by dying on the cross. He defeated the one who had the power of death, and since He has, His people will live eternally. Surely, that victroy, above all victories, is worth remembering!

For Such a Time as This

15

Mordecai Pictures Christ

*For Mordecai the Jew was next unto king Ahasuerus, and
great among the Jews, and accepted of the multitude
of his brethren, seeking the wealth of his people, and
speaking peace to all his seed.*

Esther 10:3

It would be very easy to come to the words of Esther 10 and
think of them as nothing more than an appendix or a postscript to the book. In many ways, these three brief verses appear
to record things that are routine, ordinary, and mundane. In that
sense, they are in stark contrast to the previous chapters.

Almost from the opening verse of this book there has been
drama in the Persian Empire. First the king divorced his wife and
banished her from the kingdom. Then he returned from an un-
successful campaign against the Greeks and set out to find another wife. Unknown to him, the young woman he settled on was
a Jewess, and, in the providence of God, she was brought to this

prominent position in the kingdom for a very particular reason.

Nothing happened by chance. God was at work, and He was controlling all things according to His own purposes. That truth comes more to the fore when Haman the prime minister became incensed against Mordecai the Jew and determined to kill him and all the other Jews living in Persia.

That threat was real. The law was passed by the king and the date was set. From Esther 4 to Esther 9, the narrative in God's inspired Word is one of Esther risking her life to go and plead with the king. It involves her exposing the wickedness of Haman, then his sudden and just execution on his own gallows and the passing of another law, a law permitting the Jews to defend themselves. These central chapters are full of crisis, tension, fear, plots, deaths, and eventual deliverance for the Jews.

At times, the twists and turns of these events hang on mysterious providences. God's intervention is perfect: perfect in its timing, perfect in its execution, and perfect in its results. People are where God wants them to be at the precise time He wants them to be there. When all is said and done, the divine masterpiece is perfectly woven together for God's own glory and for the good of His own people.

Esther 9 is full of war and victory. It is a chapter that records a tremendous time in the history of the Jews and in the history of Persia. There are jubilant scenes: great feasts, public and sustained thanksgiving, and the establishment of a time of joy, praise, and generosity that is still observed and repeated to this very day. Those were extraordinary days.

But if Esther 9 records extraordinary things, Esther 10 seems to revert to ordinary things. After all the drama, life in Persia returned to normal routine. Far from being merely a postscript, the detail in these three brief verses is very important. There are some simple and yet profound lessons in them.

Firstly, there is a word about life under a government or under a ruler. Verse 1 records that king Ahasuerus "laid a tribute upon the land and upon the isles of the sea." In other words, he was busy putting a taxation scheme in place, or maybe it would be better to say, *back in place*. In Esther 2:18, when he was celebrating Esther becoming his queen, he gave a tax break to the people. Now he is putting that back upon them. It is what kings do. It is how governments raise money. We may not like it, but it is part of life. Christ has told us, "Render therefore unto Caesar the things which are Caesar's; and unto God the things that are God's" (Matthew 22:21). Christ paid tribute or tax and so must we.

Secondly, there is a word here about the role of God's people in the political world. Mordecai served in the Persian Empire under Ahasuerus. Ahasuerus was a wicked man—often a drunkard, certainly arrogant, as well as proud, immoral, and bloodthirsty—everything a man should not be! Nevertheless, Mordecai had a position under him. God's people have a role to play in the life of this world. Daniel was a leader in Babylon. Obadiah served in the court of King Ahab. Godly men served in Herod's household. We ought to pray for godly men in these kinds of positions in the government of our land.

Thirdly, there is a word here about the importance of keeping good records of history. Verse 2 notes that things were recorded in the books of the Chronicles. These books were important, as seen in Esther 2:23, when someone recorded that Mordecai had exposed a plot to kill the king, and then again in Esther 6, when the king read them and honoured Mordecai for that heroic act. The proper recording of history is vital. Why? Because in it we can see the hand of God, the providence of God. History is often written with a bias; but God is always at work, and history proves that—even our own personal history. Has God not blessed you, led you, guided you? You should note these things and talk about them. Remember history, because it reveals the hand of our sovereign God. These may have been routine things, but they were very important.

But the greatest lesson of these final verses lies with the details of Mordecai and his impact in the nation and especially among the Lord's people. Throughout this book, Mordecai stands as a pivotal figure. In many ways, we can learn something of Christ as we consider his life. These verses should bring those lessons to the fore of our attention. So, in concluding the study of this book, I want to show you how Mordecai reminds me of Christ. There are four simple thoughts:

THE ADVANCEMENT OF MORDECAI

When we first meet with Mordecai in the book of Esther, he is a relatively unknown Jew living in the shadow of the palace in Shushan. Esther 2:5, 6 simply states that he was of the tribe of Benjamin and that his ancestors had been carried away captive from Jerusalem during the reign of Nebuchadnezzar. At this time, Mordecai did not occupy a prominent position in the nation. In fact, as the narrative unfolds, we learn that he was a man who was appointed to die.

Mordecai was a man of principle. He would not bow down to the Gentile Haman. Therefore he was despised, denounced, hated, and threatened. Haman sought opportunities to move against him, and went as far as order his servants to build gallows so that Mordecai could be hanged. In the eyes of Haman, and most likely in the eyes of many in Persia, this Jew was nothing more than an embarrassment. He deserved to die. It was right that he should suffer. There was nothing good about him.

Mordecai lived under a cloud of suffering and pain and rejection. However, the whole picture is reversed at the end of the book. In Esther 8, 9, and especially in Esther 10, Mordecai is no longer humiliated; he is exalted. Verse 2, speaking of Ahasuerus, records: "And all the acts of his power and his might. And the declaration of the greatness of Mordecai, whereunto the king advanced him, are they not written in the book of the chronicles of the Media and Persia?" Mordecai was noted for his greatness, and he was advanced. The word advanced means "to make large in the sense of honouring or promoting or magnifying or lifting up." That was true of Mordecai. He was lifted up and honoured by the king.

In Esther 4, he was sitting at the king's gate in sackcloth and ashes. Then, he was the man of sorrows. His heart was heavy, and he was burdened with the cares and troubles of his people. In Esther 10, he has been lifted up. His entire situation has been transformed. There is no claim of death upon him here. He lives; and he lives as an exalted and honoured man. That is seen in two ways: *His position* (v. 3): "He was next unto king Ahasuerus." That phrase may mean that his seat of prominence was literally next to the king's. It certainly means that he was viewed in a royal capacity. He was involved in the ruling or the administration of the affairs in Persia. Mordecai occupied a vital role in the kingdom. He was not sitting at the gate; he was sitting on a throne. *His power* (v. 2): "the greatness of Mordecai." The word points to his authority. We know from the end of Esther 9 that his word carried great authority in the kingdom. Mordecai had gone from being reviled to being respected. This despised Jew was advanced or exalted.

It does not take much for us to draw a straight line from Mordecai to Christ. There was a time when our Lord Jesus was the man of sorrows and the One acquainted with grief. He was despised and rejected of men. There were many who hated Him with such hatred that they plotted His death. Then, at the appointed time, He was taken to the cross, and there He died as a cursed and condemned man.

He gave up the glory of heaven and placed Himself in a state of deep humiliation. His life and death and burial all point to His awful sufferings. He was rich, but for our sakes He became poor. What humility Christ endured for His people. But He did not stay in that state, for after being under the power of death for a time, Christ arose from the dead and His humiliation gave way to His exaltation.

The tomb could not hold Him; death could not keep Him; the devil and his demons could not overcome Him; and the Roman soldiers or the Jewish leaders could not restrain Him. The hours rolled past, the stone was rolled away, and Christ came forth. Those first steps of exaltation were followed by more. He ascended back to His Father, and as the everlasting gates of glory were opened up to receive Him, the Father said to him, "Sit thou at my right hand, until I make thine enemies thy footstool." (Psalm 110)

Where is Christ today? At the Father's right hand! He is in that position of majesty, authority, and glory, and all power belongs to Him. Ahasuerus might have declared the greatness of Mordecai, but his greatness is nothing in comparison to the greatness of Christ. He lives in the power of an endless life. Christ lived and died; but He now lives for ever, and all power has been given unto Him in heaven and in earth. He is the great King of glory. He is the great Lord of lords. He is the great Mediator between God and men. He is the great Judge of all the earth. He is the great

Friend of sinners, the great Captain of His people, and the great Ruler over all men. Christ has been exalted far above all.

The world mocks this right now. But the day will come when even the ungodly will say, "Jesus Christ is Lord." Can you think of that and not be thrilled? Every knee will bow and every tongue will confess the greatness and glory of Jesus Christ. This is prefigured in the advancement of Mordecai.

THE ADMIRATION OF MORDECAI

Note the next phrase in v. 3: "For Mordecai the Jew was next unto King Ahasuerus, and great among the Jews, and accepted of the multitude of his brethren..." To put that in modern language, the Jews thought the world of Mordecai. He was accepted of his brethren. The word "accepted" is passive. In other words, it was not so much that Mordecai accepted his brethren, but that he was accepted by them—and continually accepted by them. The word "accepted" means pleased and therefore what is being stressed here is that the Jews were extremely pleased with Mordecai. They recognised his value. They appreciated him and his work. They admired his stand. He was highly esteemed by them.

If you had met a Jew in Persia and asked him, "What do you think of Mordecai? What is your opinion of him? How would you rate him?" The answer you would very likely have received would have been: "He is the greatest among all of us." Why was that the case? It was because he stood up for them. He intervened on their behalf. He stood between them and certain death at the hands of Haman. His work for them spoke volumes of his love for them, and therefore they loved him or admired him—they accepted him in return.

Do we not see a picture of Christ here? I say that for two reasons. God the Father is well pleased with Christ. He said at Christ's baptism and at Christ's transfiguration: "This is my beloved Son in whom I am well pleased" (Matthew 3:17; Matthew 17:5).

The Father is pleased with Christ; and the true believer is pleased with Christ. Go back in your mind to the question that is asked in Song of Solomon chapter 5: "What is thy beloved more than another beloved?" In response to that question, the spouse described him, then said in v. 16 "...yea, he is altogether lovely." Earlier (v. 10) she had said that he was "the chiefest of ten thousand." Are these words not appropriate concerning Christ? Peter says something similar in 1 Peter 2:7 when he notes, "Unto you therefore which believe he [Christ] is precious." This is what the believer thinks of his Deliverer. We love Him because He first loved us. We worship Him, serve Him, adore Him, and highly esteem Him. He is worthy of it all and more. There was none like Mordecai in all the Persian Empire. In a far greater sense, there is no one like Christ—our great and glorious Saviour!

Is Christ precious to you? Do you love Him? Is He the chiefest of ten thousand to your soul? What is your view of Christ? Or to take the words found in Matthew's Gospel: "What think ye of Christ?"

THE ACTIVITY OF MORDECAI

Verse 3 speaks of Mordecai as "...seeking the wealth of his people." If we take that verse as it stands, it seems to contradict the words of Esther 9:10, 15, 16, where we are told that the Jews did not take the spoil of war. In other words, they did not enrich themselves. So what does it mean that Mordecai sought the wealth of the people? The word "wealth" means good or welfare of his people. It is a much broader term. It means their safety, their good, their welfare and happiness, both temporal and spiritual.

This is what Mordecai worked for. He spent his time and energy for the good of others—taking care of them; watching out for them; making representation for them; ruling for them; dealing with their enemies; and ensuring their blessings. He sought their welfare. The word "seeking" has the idea of enquiring after. This is what Mordecai did. He was constantly before the king for the good of his people. He was their advocate, friend, benefactor, and their helper.

It is easy to see the parallel with Christ. C.H. Spurgeon said, "Mordecai was a true patriot, and therefore being exalted to the highest position under Ahasuerus, he used his eminence to promote the prosperity of Israel. In this he was a type of Jesus, who, upon His throne of glory, seeks not His own, but spends His power for His people."[12] Where is Christ, and what is He doing today? He is at the Father's right-hand pleading for His people. He is caring for His church, intervening on our behalf, ruling all things, ordering all things, and working all things for our good. He is our great exalted Saviour who bestows blessings upon us.

> *Arise, my soul, arise;*
> *Shake off thy guilty fears;*
> *The bleeding Sacrifice*
> *In my behalf appears:*
> *Before the throne my Surety stands,*
> *Before the throne my Surety stands;*
> *My name is written on His hands.*[13]

Christ is our Surety, our Advocate, our eternal and unchangeable Friend. If you are a Christian, you must understand this! He prays for you (Luke 22:30, 31; Hebrews 4:15, 16). He is there for you. That presents a timely example—and if this is what Jesus does for us, let us do it for each other. As C.H. Spurgeon said,

> Every Christian should be a Mordecai to the Church, striving according to his ability for its prosperity. Some are placed in stations of affluence and influence; let them testify for Jesus before great men. Others have what is far better, namely, close fellowship with the King of kings; let them be sure to plead daily for the weak of the Lord's people, the doubting, the tempted, and the comfortless. The very least in our Israel may at least seek the welfare of his people; and his desire, if he can give no more, shall be acceptable. It is at once the most Christlike and the most happy course for a believer to cease from living to himself. He who blesses others cannot fail to be blessed himself. On the other hand, to seek our own personal greatness is a wicked and unhappy plan of life; its way will be grievous and its end will be fatal.[14]

12   *Devotional Classics of C H Spurgeon*, (Evening Reading: "Seeking the Welfare of His People—Esther 10:3) 28. https://books.google.com/books?isbn=1589601661

13   *Arise, my soul, arise*, Charles Wesley

14   *Devotional Classics of C H Spurgeon*, *Ibid*

The Assurance from Mordecai

The book of Esther closes with Mordecai speaking peace to all his seed. This was a tremendous change from the central chapters of the book. The Jews in Persia had faced war, trouble, and turmoil; Mordecai brought a message of peace.

There is an interesting phrase in Esther 9:20 which outlines that Mordecai had sent letters to all the Jews, across the 127 provinces of Persia, both near and far. In v. 30 of the same chapter, we discover details of another letter that was sent to all the Jews, with words of peace and truth.

The peace that Mordecai sought for his people extended far and near, and it was a peace based upon truth. Furthemore it was sent to all people in the realm. The written word confirmed his work for and assurance to the people.

There is a gospel picture in these words. When Christ was born, angels brought the message of His birth to shepherds in the fields outside Bethlehem. Their message to those humble shepherds was powerful, extensive, and glorious. The details are recorded in Luke 2:8-14:

> And there were in the same country shepherds abiding in the field, keeping watch over their flock by night. And, lo, the angel of the Lord came upon them, and the glory of the Lord shone round about them: and they were sore afraid. And the angel said unto them, Fear not: for, behold, I bring you good tidings of great joy, which shall be to all people. For unto you is born this day in the city of David a Saviour, which is Christ the Lord. And this shall be a sign unto you; Ye shall find the babe wrapped in swaddling clothes, lying in a manger. And suddenly there was with the angel a multitude of the heavenly host praising God, and saying, Glory to God in the highest, and on earth peace, good will toward men.

The angels' message concurred with the Old Testament message of Isaiah 57:19, "I create the fruit of the lips; Peace, peace to him that is afar off, and to him that is near, saith the Lord; and

I will heal him." The gospel message of peace with God through the Lord Jesus Christ is for those far and near. The gospel is for everyone. Christ secures peace through the blood of His cross, and peace is promised to all who come unto Him in faith.

*

Esther and Mordecai and all the Jews in Persia at that time are gone. The king is no longer on his throne. The Persian empire has been replaced. The world has moved on and new rulers have come and gone. However, the God whose name does not appear in this book is still on the throne in glory. Christ is still the Head and only King of His people and He is continuing to build His church. There are times when it seems things are going against God's people. The enemies of the gospel appear strong and almost invincible. At times the situation in the world almost overwhelms the godly man but only when he forgets that God is still in control of all things, even as He was in the time of Esther. We have one greater than Mordecai; we have Christ, and since God is for us, who can be against us? The brief book of Esther provides us with a glimpse of the power and grace of God. The Scriptures are full of such glimpses, because the Scriptures are full of Christ. Believers can take heart, for Christ is our Beloved and our Friend.

About the Author

Colin Mercer was converted to Christ at a young age. Following several years in employment as an accounts clerk, he entered the Whitefield College of the Bible to train for the gospel ministry within the Free Presbyterian Church of Ulster. He has pastored churches in Castlederg and Kilkeel (Northern Ireland), and Greenville (USA) before taking up his present charge in Omagh, (Northern Ireland). Colin is married to Heather. They have two daughters, Lois, who lives in USA with her husband Miles, and Hannah, who resides in Belfast, Northern Ireland.